The Art of Flourishing

The Art of Flourishing

Conversations on Disability

Edited by
LIZ BOWEN
JOEL MICHAEL REYNOLDS
ROSEMARIE GARLAND-THOMSON
ERIK PARENS

OXFORD
UNIVERSITY PRESS

Oxford University Press is a department of the University of Oxford.
It furthers the University's objective of excellence in research, scholarship,
and education by publishing worldwide. Oxford is a registered trade mark of
Oxford University Press in the UK and in certain other countries.

Published in the United States of America by Oxford University Press
198 Madison Avenue, New York, NY 10016, United States of America.

© Oxford University Press 2025

All rights reserved. No part of this publication may be reproduced, stored in a retrieval system, transmitted, used for text and data mining, or used for training artificial intelligence, in any form or by any means, without the prior permission in writing of Oxford University Press, or as expressly permitted by law, by license or under terms agreed with the appropriate reprographics rights organization. Inquiries concerning reproduction outside the scope of the above should be sent to the Rights Department, Oxford University Press, at the address above.

You must not circulate this work in any other form
and you must impose this same condition on any acquirer

CIP data is on file at the Library of Congress

ISBN 9780197625712 (Pbk.)
ISBN 9780197625705 (hbk.)

DOI: 10.1093/9780197625743.001.0001

The manufacturer's authorised representative in the EU for product safety is Oxford University Press España S.A. of El Parque Empresarial San Fernando de Henares, Avenida de Castilla, 2 – 28830 Madrid (www.oup.es/en or product.safety@oup.com). OUP España S.A. also acts as importer into Spain of products made by the manufacturer.

*With gratitude for the life and teaching of Adrienne Asch (1946–2013),
a pioneering disability rights activist and the first bioethicist to successfully demand that the field of bioethics listen to the disability critique.*

Contents

Preface ix
Acknowledgments xi
List of Contributors xiii

    Introduction 1
    Liz Bowen, Joel Michael Reynolds, Rosemarie
    Garland-Thomson, and Erik Parens

1. Belonging: On Disability, Technology, and Community 11
   Haben Girma, Rachel Kolb, and Teresa Blankmeyer Burke

2. Navigating: On Disability, Technology, and
Experiencing the World 34
   Yomi Sachiko Young, Rod Michalko, and Kim Q. Hall

3. Disrupting Ableism with Artful Activism 69
   Lateef McLeod and D.J. Savarese

4. Questioning Cure: Disability, Identity, and Healing 103
   Anand Prahlad, Ann Millett-Gallant, and
   Karen Nakamura

5. Enjoying: Disability as a Creative Force 140
   Julia Watts Belser, Georgina Kleege, and Jerron Herman

6. We Belong to One Another: Disability and
Family-Making 175
   Jina Kim, Jess Waggoner, Sami Schalk, Joseph Stramondo,
   Leah Smith, and Mia Mingus

Notes 211

Preface

The Brilliant Brain Flowers of Katherine Sherwood

Rosemarie Garland-Thomson

The brain of the artist and educator, Katherine Sherwood, unexpectedly exploded one day during the prime of her life, transforming her body, mind, and—perhaps most significant—her right hand. That cerebral hemorrhage put an end to her art practice as it had been during her career as an accomplished artist and professor at the University of California, Berkeley. During her long medical treatment and rehabilitation, Sherwood encountered myriad medical images of her own brain that her neurology team was intently examining. She came to understand that the medical images of her brain she viewed in the darkened clinic were portraits of her face rendered in an aesthetic form she had not considered before in her artistic practice. Sherwood came also to recognize that this image of her brain transformed by the cerebral hemorrhage that reshaped her body could also reshape her artistic practice. She began to paint with her left hand, changing both the way she made art and the art she made. Just as the hemorrhage had impressed itself on her body, she imprinted her new body onto her art. Sherwood incorporates this distinctive signature of her brain image on every work of art she now makes. From the faces of her Odalisques and ample nudes to the floral still lives and the more recent Madonnas, Sherwood embeds her own image signature, her distinctive medical cameo, into all her art.

We find Sherwood's brain images tucked into the buds of emergent flowers, nested in the spent blooms, entangled in the winding stems, and hidden in the leafy profusions of her flower still life paintings.

We offer you on our cover Katherine Sherwood's *Butterfly and Birds (After Giovanna Garzoni)*, one of her 2024 series of flower still life paintings. *Butterfly and Birds* draws together several aesthetic traditions to tell the story about human flourishing that all of Sherwood's art gives us. The explosion in Katherine Sherwood's brain that transformed her body and her art comes to us in *Butterfly and Birds* as an explosion of painterly practices honoring human flourishing. The painting brings together a wide color palette of symmetry amid asymmetry in a rich floral tapestry of intertwined vines, flowers, birds, bugs, snails, and caterpillars, in lively yet orderly profusion. Dotted with Sherwood's signature brain images, some obvious and others obscure, the painting is a visual story of her own capacious brain and nature's wondrous abundance. Sherwood's flowers, butterflies, birds, crawling things, and brains converge in a tangle of aesthetic references that at once delight and caution us about the frailty and durability of human embodied life. Sherwood gathers painterly traditions ranging from the vanitas themes of vigilant mortality reminding us that all things human perish to the Dutch still lives of early modern era that celebrate carnal human life. The garden of delights amid warnings in *Butterfly and Birds* announces and anticipates the stories of flourishing that each chapter of our book presents. Katherine Sherwood's paintings are testimonies to disability resourcefulness; with them, we extend to you *The Art of Flourishing*.

Acknowledgments

We acknowledge Sana Baban, Sophie Pollack-Milgate, and Luis Daniel Acevedo-Vélez for doing the crucially important work of preparing the manuscript for publication; our program officer at the National Endowment for the Humanities, Patricia Brooks, for supporting the project from the very start; the Public Humanities Projects program at NEH for enabling us to create the series of public conversations on which this volume is based; and former Hastings Center president, Mildred Solomon, and current president, Vardit Ravitsky, for providing additional funds required to curate the series and create this book. All proceeds from this volume will be donated to disability arts and justice organizations.

Contributors

Julia Watts Belser, PhD, is Professor of Jewish Studies and Disability Studies, Department of Theology and Religious Studies, Georgetown University, Washington, DC, USA.

Liz Bowen, PhD, is Assistant Professor, Center for Bioethics and Humanities, SUNY Upstate Medical University, Syracuse, NY, USA.

Teresa Blankmeyer Burke, PhD, is Professor of Philosophy, Director of the School of Arts & Humanities, Gallaudet University, Washington, DC, USA.

Rosemarie Garland-Thomson, PhD, is Professor Emerita of English and Bioethics, Emory University, Atlanta, GA, USA.

Haben Girma, JD, is an independent author and advocate, CA, USA.

Kim Q. Hall, PhD, is Professor of Philosophy, University of Alberta, Alberta, CA.

Jerron Herman, BA, is a choreographer, dancer, and interdisciplinary artist.

Jina Kim, PhD, is Assistant Professor of English and the Study of Women, Gender, and Sexuality, Smith College, Northampton, MA, USA.

Georgina Kleege is Professor Emerita, English, University of California, Berkeley, Berkeley, CA, USA.

Rachel Kolb, PhD, is Junior Fellow, Society of Fellows, Harvard University, Cambridge, MA, USA.

Lateef McLeod, MFA, PhD, is a graduating grad student, Anthropology and Social Change, California Institute of Integral Studies, San Francisco and Oakland, CA, USA.

Rod Michalko, PhD, is retired Professor, University of Toronto, Toronto, CA.

Ann E. Millett, PhD, is Senior Lecturer, Bachelor of Arts in Liberal and Professional Studies, University of North Carolina at Greensboro, Greensboro, NC, USA.

Mia Mingus is a writer, educator, and trainer for transformative justice and disability justice.

Karen Nakamura, PhD, is Haas Distinguished Chair in Disability Studies and Professor of Anthropology, University of California Berkeley, Berkeley, CA, USA.

Erik Parens, PhD, is a senior research scholar, The Hastings Center, Garrison, NY, USA.

Anand Prahlad is Curators' Distinguished Teaching Professor Emeritus, Department of English and Thompson Center for Autism and Neurodevelopment, University of Missouri, Columbia, MO, USA.

Joel Michael Reynolds, PhD, is Associate Professor of Philosophy and Disability Studies, Georgetown University, Washington, DC, USA.

David James Savarese, BA, is Co-Chair, The Alliance for Citizen Directed Supports, Media, PA, USA.

Sami Schalk, PhD, is Professor of Gender and Women's Studies, University of Wisconsin-Madison, Madison, WI, USA.

Leah Smith, MPA, is Associate Director, The National Center for Disability, Equity, and Intersectionality, San Diego, CA, USA.

Joseph A. Stramondo, PhD, is Associate Professor of Philosophy and Humanities, San Diego State University, San Diego, CA, USA.

Jess Waggoner, PhD, is Assistant Professor in Gender and Women's Studies and English, University of Wisconsin-Madison, Madison, WI, USA.

Yomi Sachiko Young, BA, is a writer, activist, and disability justice dreamer, Oakland, CA, USA.

Introduction

*Liz Bowen, Joel Michael Reynolds,
Rosemarie Garland-Thomson, and Erik Parens*

"We can define disability as an opportunity for innovation. If you can't do something one way, come up with a new, innovative way to do that thing."

To some, this statement by Haben Girma in Chapter 1 of this book might be as intuitive as the idea that human diversity and creativity enrich our lives. To others, it might be revolutionary to imagine that disability, an experience most people are taught to fear, could entail things most people are taught to value, such as opportunity and innovation. *The Art of Flourishing: Conversations on Disability* welcomes all these readers, from those who may be seeking a deeper understanding of disability for the first time—whether out of a sense of justice, curiosity, or a newly acquired identity—to those who have spent decades enmeshed in disability culture and community. Disability is often defined in terms of its openness and heterogeneity: anyone can become disabled at any time, and there is a world of difference encompassed within it. This means that disability communities tend to be populated with newcomers as well as seasoned mentors, and everyone is a learner.

Anyone who has spent time in a disability community can attest to the excitement of these learnings: the thrill of learning a new hack for making a previously inaccessible object useful, for example, or the pleasure of learning to engage with artworks across a range of sensory modes. Disabled people are experts in innovation and adaptation, experts in building networks of support and knowledge sharing, and experts in navigating a world that is not built for them. This expertise is not a niche form of knowledge, but one that speaks to the fundamental question about how we should live together—and even thrive together—amid the vast landscape of human difference. In pieces discussing everything from moving with guide dogs to hiking on wheels to nurturing chosen family, this volume offers a window into the innumerable ways people with disabilities understand what it means to flourish. The heart of this book comes in the form of the following proclamation:

> *People can flourish in all sorts of bodyminds. To flourish means to exercise the capacities we have in pursuit of the goals we find meaningful. None of us needs a different bodymind to flourish. What we need is more supportive environments.*

We live in a moment of heightened awareness about disability as a cultural and political identity, with an unprecedented proliferation of popular media that represent experiences of disability from the perspective of disabled people. The disability activism documentary *Crip Camp* (2020) was not only nominated for an Oscar but also has become essential viewing in schools and universities across the United States, as has Alice Wong's rich and multilayered anthology of first-person narratives *Disability Visibility*, and the collection of essays edited by Peter Catapano and Rosemarie Garland-Thomson *About Us: Essays from the "New York Times" about Disability by People with Disabilities*. Moreover, social media platforms like TikTok and Instagram have enabled self-advocates from numerous disability communities to connect with each other and with broader publics. Whereas, even five years ago, it would have been a surprise to see concepts such as "neurodiversity" and "ableism" being addressed outside activist or academic circles, these are now terms that circulate widely in families, schools, and workplaces.

At the same time, even such broad public awareness has its limits. As algorithmic social media platforms have become even more ideologically siloed than traditional media outlets, it is rare that what is highly present in one demographic will be prominent everywhere else. Indeed, in some of the areas that hold the highest stakes for disabled people, such as the healthcare system, outdated and damaging assumptions and language about disability and disabled people still reign. People with disabilities routinely report negative experiences of healthcare, including medical trauma, as a result of common manifestations of ableism, including: having all new symptoms erroneously attributed to their disability, being refused an appointment because of access barriers, being injured by staff during transfers, being treated like a rare specimen rather than a patient, being ignored while the provider talks only to the patient's companion, being assumed asexual or incompetent, or being discouraged from having children.

While some of these negative experiences arise from physical barriers or inadequate medical and/or legal knowledge, others testify to limited imaginations about the wide range of possibilities that a life with a disability can give us. All four editors of this volume work in the field of bioethics, a field that is deeply entwined with the healthcare system, and some of us are disabled. We share a profound frustration with the harmful and inaccurate imaginaries that have taken root under the presumed authority of medicine and, moreover, that have come to represent bioethics in the minds of many who have been harmed as a result of those imaginaries. We also share a hope that bioethics can offer more rigorous approaches to thinking about flourishing, building on the long history of bioethicists, some of them disabled, who have challenged their colleagues to take seriously the insights of disability activism and disability studies.[1] We believe that, by listening to what the disabled people in this volume say flourishing consists in for them, bioethicists—and others—can grow their imaginations and deepen their understanding of what flourishing means.

Indeed, the authority for determining what specific capacities are required for life to be meaningful or enjoyable should lie with disabled people themselves. We know from our own and others' experiences that there is no one capacity, or set of capacities, that can truly be said to either guarantee or preclude human flourishing. Instead, we again propose that flourishing takes place when people exercise their own capacities in ways they find meaningful. And while the meanings of flourishing are highly personal and resist generalization, there are still important lessons that we all would do well to heed when it comes to disability and flourishing. Many people experience flourishing not when they are cured of a disability, for instance, but when they have the autonomy to make their own decisions about how they move through the world, when they feel supported in both the use and refusal of adaptive devices, and when they have access to social belonging and community.

It is these multifaceted possibilities that we aimed to illuminate in our webinar series: *The Art of Flourishing: Conversations on Disability*, which encompassed six public conversations between 2019 and 2022, generously funded by the National Endowment for the Humanities. These conversations brought together disabled artists, activists, scholars, and thought leaders of diverse backgrounds and identities in order to help more people think about how truly varied and unpredictable flourishing can be. Initially, our focus was narrow, as we conceived of these conversations with a focus on technology, asking, When do technological advancements support the flourishing of people with disabilities and when do they inhibit it? But it quickly became clear that our collaborating presenters had a lot to say about the very meaning of flourishing that extended far beyond that starting question, and that sometimes rendered questions about technology beside the point.

Each event's theme evolved organically out of multiple conversations among the presenters in the format that best suited their needs, and while some, like "Navigating" in Chapter 2, directly addressed the impacts of certain medical technologies on the lives of disabled people, others dispensed with the notion that technology should be a primary area of focus even in areas where, historically, technologies have been subjected to strong critique from disability advocates. For instance, in the "Family-Making" conversation of Chapter 6, presenters expanded the focus beyond reproductive technologies like prenatal genetic testing—a long-running point of debate among disability activists and among bioethicists—toward an inquiry into how the broadly limiting model of the nuclear family has contributed to ableist ideas about who should be a parent.

Still, the theme of technology's affordances and risks did not leave us, but rather became a live element of our work together. Only our first event, "On Belonging" of Chapter 1, was held primarily in person with a livestream, as the series was initially conceived. When we had to recalibrate after the onset of the COVID-19 pandemic, we found that the format of an entirely virtual webinar opened up our reach far beyond the project's original ambitions. Whereas our first event had about one hundred people in the audience with a few people on the livestream, our first webinar, "Navigating" of Chapter 2, drew more than seven hundred live viewers from a wide range of backgrounds, including disability community members, healthcare professionals, and bioethics scholars. As many people with disabilities noted at the time, the shift to virtual gatherings expanded accessibility in many ways, allowing people to attend events they previously might not have attended because of barriers like inaccessible public transit or caregiving responsibilities.

At the same time, it soon became clear that expanded accessibility in one sphere came with new access barriers in others. In the early days of Zoom's ascension to ubiquitous popular use, its support resources offered little to no guidance on how to use its very limited accessibility features. The closed captioning tool had major bugs that caused some participants not to be able to see captions during webinars, and the spotlighting tool often failed to keep sign language interpreters in view during screen sharing. Meanwhile, individual access needs sometimes clashed over virtual communication. Some people needed to communicate primarily or only via the chat function, while others could not see or type in the chat. The truncated view of the Zoom square flattened the embodied and visual aspects of some disabilities, such that some people who were visibly disabled in physical settings were no longer visibly disabled in virtual space. None of these tensions was impossible to resolve, but they required significant flexibility, creativity, and benefit of the doubt when obstacles arose.

People with disabilities are no strangers to these skills and practices. As Karen Nakamura puts it in Chapter 4, disabled flourishing often means hacking the world to make it work for bodyminds it was not designed to work for. And we cannot do it alone. Perhaps no word emerged more over the course of our six conversations than "interdependence." The conversations in this collection reveal the many ways in which embracing interdependence can mean grappling with conflicting access needs and navigating uncomfortable power dynamics, but they also make abundantly clear how recognizing interdependence can open up deep experiences of connection and joy. There is no flourishing without interdependence.

This book and the conversations within it are organized into six kinds of activity that, for our groups of presenters, are involved in the pursuit of flourishing: Belonging, Navigating, Disrupting, Questioning, Enjoying, and Making. In Chapter 1, "Belonging: On Disability, Technology, and Community," three pathbreaking Deaf scholars and advocates explored how assistive and medical technology has both expanded access for Deaf and disabled people *and* carried the potential for diminishing human diversity. Haben Girma, the first Deafblind person to graduate from Harvard Law School, tells the story of how fighting for accessible technology on her college campus taught her about the power of advocacy for herself and others. Writer and disability advocate Rachel Kolb, who was the first Deaf Rhodes scholar at Oxford, discusses her decision to obtain a cochlear implant while maintaining a Deaf identity, illustrating how the use of the technology can coexist both with the embodied experience of deafness and with cultural belonging in Deaf community. Bioethicist Teresa Blankmeyer Burke, who was the first signing Deaf woman in the world to receive a PhD in philosophy, examines the implications of gene-editing technology for human diversity and the tensions that can arise between how parents think about what is best for their children versus what might be best for the world.

Chapter 2, "Navigating: On Disability, Technology, and Experiencing the World," foregrounds the idea that being able to choose how one moves through the world is an essential component of a flourishing life. Disability justice activist Yomi Sachiko Young revisits a moment in childhood when she learned a hard truth about access to mobility equipment being central to identity development, revealing what happens when assistive technology is stripped away from or foisted on a person. Rod Michalko, a blind sociologist, describes how moving with his guide dog Smokie allowed him to experience the world in new ways, and even created a world unto the two of them. Kim Q. Hall, a philosopher, shares a narrative in which queerness and childhood surgery come together to shape a limping-swaggering mode of navigating the world, troubling the distinction between disability and ability.

The poet-activists in Chapter 3, "Disrupting Ableism with Artful Activism," demonstrate how collaborative and justice-oriented work in the arts can help us both imagine a world led by people with disabilities and bring that world into being through creative forms of resistance. Lateef McLeod, a PhD candidate in anthropology and social change, imagines a revolutionary change effort in which liberation comes not through assistive devices or policy, but through constructing new cultural narratives that emphasize the "full, multi-faceted humanity of people with disabilities." D.J.

Savarese, poet and coproducer of the documentary *Deej: Inclusion Shouldn't Be a Lottery* (2017), explains how autism has given him a visceral sense of the world's interconnectedness, which has fundamentally shaped his collaborative artistic endeavors aimed at unsettling preconceived narratives about disability.

Chapter 4, "Questioning Cure: Disability, Identity, and Healing," asks whether cure should be the ultimate aim of healthcare, pointing toward the ways in which the medical establishment's pursuit of cure can be at the expense of other goals that disabled people might prioritize, such as exploring a disability identity, making the current world more accessible, or working toward various kinds of personal and societal healing. Folklorist and poet Anand Prahlad uncovers the intimately entwined histories of racism and ableism in constructing cure as a fairytale of transformation into a "white, so-called normal," arguing that it is society that needs to be cured of its exploitative and individualist myths. Art historian and visual artist Ann Millett-Gallant reflects on how fostering her artistic practice following a traumatic brain injury has enabled her to pursue healing without the prospect of, or need for, a cure. Karen Nakamura, a cultural and visual anthropologist, contrasts the notion of cure with that of "hacking the world," showcasing the ways disabled people alter physical space and leave historical traces that testify to the existence and significance of disability culture.

In Chapter 5, "Enjoying: Disability as a Creative Force," disabled artists and writers explore the nature of disabled joy: what it means to feel pleasure, abundance, creative energy, and fulfillment because of—not despite—disability. Rabbi and scholar Julia Watts Belser invites us into the particular pleasures of hiking with a wheelchair, showing how disabled encounters with the land can engender insights into ecology, beauty, and interdependence. Georgina Kleege, a scholar of blindness and visual art, introduces herself as a haptic docent who communicates the experience of touching artworks to others, "bring[ing] blindness into the museum" as a form of art appreciation. Dancer and writer Jerron Herman shares a piece of video art in which disabled dancers enjoy the warmth and cacophony of a dinner party, locating creativity and pleasure in disabled aesthetics like a stall, a stutter, or a misstep.

The conversation that concludes the volume, "We Belong to One Another: Disability and Family-Making," brings together the series' largest group of writers, activists, and scholars to discuss how disability can create new opportunities for flourishing by offering alternatives to traditional notions of what family is and should be. Critical disability studies scholars Jina Kim, Sami Schalk, and Jess Waggoner offer a series of vignettes into their lives as queercrip doulas for the young people in their lives who are navigating new identities as queer, trans, and disabled. Bioethicist Joseph Stramondo and disability rights advocate Leah Smith use the concept of disability gain to describe both the embodied and social benefits that disability can bring to the practice of parenting, reflecting what their experience as disabled coparents has offered their family. Finally, writer and disability justice organizer Mia Mingus explores the possibilities and limitations of disabled kinship through the lens of what she calls access intimacy, or the feeling of belonging that arises when someone understands your access needs on an intuitive level.

Even as people who have lived and studied with disability for many years, we regularly found our own thinking and practices pushed in new directions by the participants in the *Art of Flourishing* project. Our hope is that these rich and dynamic talks can continue to generate new teaching, learning, and creation, and serve as an archive of the truly singular moment in which they entered the world. As we move from a period of generally recognized crisis and collective care in 2020 to a reinstatement of business-as-usual individualism, many disabled people remain vulnerable to the effects of COVID-19 while long COVID continues to render millions of people newly disabled.[2] It is essential to preserve evidence that things can be and have been otherwise. Though what we offer here is only one small piece of that history, we believe it is such evidence. These conversations show that under unimaginable circumstances, interdependence is both a necessity and an opening to new ways of being and flourishing. They compel us to ask, in the words of Anand Prahlad:

"How can I flourish if all the *me*s aren't?"

1

Belonging

On Disability, Technology, and Community

Haben Girma, Rachel Kolb, and Teresa Blankmeyer Burke

Erik Parens:

Thank you so much for joining the first in our series of six events called *The Art of Flourishing: Conversations on Disability, Technology, and Belonging*. My name is Erik Parens. I'm a senior research scholar at the Hastings Center, which is a bioethics research institute in Garrison, New York. The primary funder of this series is the National Endowment for the Humanities, but this series would not have come into being without the generous in-kind support offered by The Hastings Center's president, Millie Solomon.

This series has two overarching aims. The first is to broadcast a basic but profound point, which is that people can flourish in all sorts of bodies. That is, the flourishing of persons does not depend upon their having any one particular sort of body. Rather, it depends on their having the opportunities to exercise the capacities of the body that they were born with. When people can freely exercise their capacities in pursuit of their goals, they can be said to flourish.[1] People don't need different bodies to flourish. They need different, more supportive environments.

Our second aim is to explore a basic but profound question: What can all of us learn from how people with disabilities are, in their efforts to flourish, using or resisting the use of emerging technologies? Indeed, on the one hand, people with disabilities are often on the leading edge of creating and using new technologies to promote their own flourishing. On the other hand, people with disabilities have been among the most outspoken critics of some emerging technologies, notably genetic technologies that aim to influence the sorts of bodies that babies are born with.

Our first speaker tonight, Haben Girma, is a Deafblind lawyer who advocates for equal opportunities for people with disabilities, and Haben will describe how technologies have been a crucial element in her efforts to flourish.

Our second speaker, Rachel Kolb, is a Deaf scholar of English literature and disability studies, who, in addition to using American Sign Language (ASL), uses a cochlear implant. Rachel will explain how using ASL alongside a cochlear implant allows her to be a member of the Deaf and hearing communities.

Our third speaker, Teresa Blankmeyer Burke, is a Deaf professor of philosophy at Gallaudet who will invite us to think about new gene-editing technologies that in principle could be used to select against or for traits like deafness. Teresa will invite us to ask whether an environment in which parents can choose what sorts of bodies their children will have would, in fact, be a better environment for those children.

All three of our speakers tonight share an unshakable commitment to creating a society where we use technologies in ways that support many very different ways of flourishing. The question surely is not, "Are we in general for or against technology?" I don't think that's a helpful question. The question is, "How can we wisely use technologies in ways that enable all of us to flourish?" So, it is now my pleasure to turn the microphone over to Haben Girma. Again, thank you very much for coming tonight.

Haben Girma:

Good evening, everyone. Thank you, Erik, for the welcome. My name is Haben Girma, and I work as an advocate for people with disabilities. I'm also the author of a new book called *Haben: The Deafblind Woman Who Conquered Harvard Law*. Harvard has not been the same since.

Before I got there, I had to understand: What does Deafblindness mean? Deafblindness is a spectrum of vision and hearing loss. And we in the Deafblind community use lots of different techniques and strategies for communication. Some sign visually. Some sign through tactile, through touch. Others use print on palm, where they write letters on palms; and me, I had to figure out what can I do to best access information. When I was growing up with Deafblindness, I was excluded from a lot of information. The schools I attended were sighted, hearing schools in a sighted, hearing society, and I missed out on a lot of information, even within my family. I experienced isolation, and it's frustrating to feel that. And I wondered, "Do Deafblind people just tolerate this? Is this just part of being disabled, accepting inferior experiences, less access?" Then I asked myself, "What are my strengths?"

One of my strengths is my sense of touch. In first grade, I learned braille, and I've been using braille all my life. Then in 2010, a new braille device came out. Humanware produced the first real braille notebook with Bluetooth support. I'm holding up the device. There's braille on the bottom. I run my fingers over the dots to feel the letters. I found that if I connected this device to a keyboard, I can hand people the keyboard and they can type and I'll read their words. Most people in my family and community don't know braille, don't know how to sign. But most of them can type, especially millennials.

So, throughout this presentation, this is the system I'm going to be using. There are typists in the front row, typing on a keyboard, and I'm reading the words in braille. I want to stay connected with the audience. Everyone needs connection. All humans need to find a way to form friendships, connect with family. And now I have a way to connect with the audience. So, they're letting me know when people smile, laugh, fall asleep. They're watching you.

The name Haben comes from Eritrea. It's a small African country. It borders Ethiopia to the south, and to the north is the Red Sea. My mother grew up during the war between Eritrea and Ethiopia. There was a lot of violence and a lot of fear. Schools were places for students to come together and hear stories from around the world. Stories are powerful. Stories influence the organizations we design, the products we build, and the futures we imagine for ourselves.

My mother heard stories that America is the land of opportunities, the land of civil rights. These stories inspired her to take a dangerous journey, walking from Eritrea to Sudan, and it took about three weeks to do that walk. She was in Sudan for about 10 months when a refugee organization helped her come to the United States. Several years later, older and wiser, my mother realized it's not geography that creates justice. It's people that create justice. Communities create justice. All of us face the choice to accept unfairness or advocate for justice. As the daughter of refugees, a Black woman, and disabled, lots of stories say my life doesn't matter. I choose to resist those stories. My parents heard from the Ethiopian-Eritrean community, "Poor thing, she won't get a job; she won't go to school," and they had to learn to resist those stories. We found instead that we can define disability as an opportunity for innovation. If you can't do something one way, come up with a new, innovative way to do that thing.

People with disabilities have been doing this all throughout history. These are hidden stories. Many people in the mainstream don't know these stories. We have to get these stories out there, so that the public realizes that disability can be an opportunity for innovation. We have challenges, but we also have talents.

Technology plays a tremendous role in increasing opportunities for people with disabilities, but only if it's designed to be accessible. My computer will allow me to connect with people, if people choose to meet me halfway. I've had people say, "No, that's strange. That's weird," and walk away. And that creates the barrier. We've also had people develop technologies that are not accessible. For most of my life, I could enter an elevator, read the button in braille, select the button, and step out when I get to my floor. Now I'm encountering elevators that are all touch screens and not accessible to blind individuals. So, a freedom I used to have, to freely move around a building, has been taken away by technology.

People who develop tech should design with access in mind so they can reach the largest number of people. There are over a billion people with disabilities around the world. When you design tech to be accessible, you get more customers, people with disabilities, their families, their communities. So, I'm hopeful that more people in tech will design with access in mind, or risk litigation.

Now I'm going to share a story from my book. When I decided to become an advocate, it was a slow process, and it started when I was in college. I went to Lewis and Clark College in Portland, Oregon, and at Lewis and Clark they love their pioneers. Everything is called "pioneers." The football team is The Pioneers. Their bus is the Pioneer Express, and the bus takes you to Pioneer Square. I thought maybe this would be a place that celebrates difference, a place where I can pioneer my way through the unknown. The college did a great job providing me all my course books in braille. The exams were in braille. They even worked with the Outdoor Club so I could have access to rock climbing and kayaking.

There was just one problem. The college cafeteria was a place for students to go in, eat, and relax between classes. It's in a large room and as you enter along three of the walls were panoramic windows showcasing Portland's rain. And on the fourth wall were food stations. Sighted students would walk in, browse the print menu, then go to their station of choice. I couldn't read the menu, not because of blindness, but because of the format of the menu. So, I went to the cafeteria manager and explained, "I can't read print, but I can read. Can you provide the menu in braille or posted online or email it to me? I have assistive technology that allows me to read e-mail and websites."

The manager said, "We're very busy. We have over a thousand students. We don't have time to do special things for students with special needs." Just to be clear: eating is not a special need. Everyone needs to eat.

There's this myth that there are two kinds of people: independent and dependent. It's not true. We're all interdependent. Many of you like drinking coffee. I bet very few of you grow your own coffee beans. You depend on other people to grow your food and build your technology. That's okay, as long as we're honest about the fact that we're all interdependent. Everyone at some point needs to depend on other people.

The manager of the cafeteria didn't understand this. I was a vegetarian back then, and it was hard to eat vegetarian when you don't know what the food choices are. There were about six different stations. I'd go to one at random, get food, find a table, try the food and discover an unpleasant surprise. It was really frustrating, but I told myself, "At least I had food. Many people around the world struggled for food. Why should I complain?"

My mother, when she was my age, was a refugee in Sudan. At least I was outside of the war. At least I was getting an education at a college here. Maybe I should just be grateful. We engage in the oppression Olympics, where we compare struggles, point to someone, and say, "Their struggles are worse. Therefore, I need to stop complaining and just be grateful." That's not helpful.

When you do that, you accommodate institutions. You allow problems to persist. So, I talked to friends, did research. Then I went back to the cafeteria manager and explained, "The Americans with Disabilities Act prohibits discrimination, and if you don't provide access to the menu, I'm taking legal action." I had no idea how to do that. And I was just nineteen. I couldn't afford a lawyer. Now I know there are nonprofit legal centers that help students with disabilities. But back then, I didn't know that. All I knew was I had to try, had to do something.

The next day, the manager apologized and promised to make the menus accessible. He did. He kept his word. They started emailing me the menus. Life became delicious. The next year, a new blind student came to the college, and he had immediate access to the menus. That taught me that when I advocate, I help everyone who comes after me.

There are many barriers in our community, lots of small barriers, and sometimes we tell ourselves, "Just tolerate it. Don't complain." But that's not helpful. All of you face the choice to accept unfairness or advocate for justice. When you take the time to address the small barriers, you build up the skills to master the larger obstacles. Tech has helped me throughout my life, but, more than tech, it is people doing the work to dismantle barriers that truly creates access and allows the disabled to flourish. My name, Haben, means "pride" in the language Tigrinya. A lot of people are ashamed of difference, ashamed of disability. I want to create a culture where everyone celebrates difference, where we have disability pride. The stories we tell ourselves about disability shape our culture and shape our access. Let's work to create a world where everyone has access to the tools that allow them to flourish. And now I'm going to pass it on to an amazing speaker and scholar. Let's hear it for Rachel.

Rachel Kolb:

(**Spoken**) Okay, thank you all. Hearing people. Can you hear me? Thumbs up? Good. I can't rely on myself with that. Thank you for having me here today. I remember pretty distinctively the first day that I started thinking about getting a cochlear implant. It was almost exactly ten years ago: October of 2009. I was a sophomore in college. I'd just gotten home after a long and frustrating day. It was the kind of day that other Deaf and hard-of-hearing people in this room will immediately recognize. It was the kind of day when all my hearing friends talked too fast, interrupted each other, switched conversation topics, then suddenly all burst into laughter. When I asked what was going on, they said, "Oh, everything's fine. We'll tell you later."

I went home and wondered, "What am I even doing? How am I going to live in this hearing world for the rest of my life?"

This feeling was not new, but I had always figured out new ways to navigate it. Later, I would figure out even more new strategies, including picking more friends who can sign. But that day I was still young, and I was also seeing how profoundly the world was not made for Deaf people like me. I knew communication was my right, but how was I supposed to access communication if most people spoke and heard? So that day in 2009, the thought came into my mind for the first time. *What if I got a cochlear implant?* Could that be a way to make some things easier, sometimes? Right away, the very idea felt like a betrayal. It felt like a betrayal of the larger Deaf community, too, and for the sake of the conversation we're going to have tonight, I want to explain why.

We sometimes frame conversations that we have about ourselves and our communities, but also the technology we all use, too simply and absolutely. Culturally Deaf people have, sometimes with good reason, perceived cochlear implants as technology that involves deeply problematic able-bodied ideas of medical care and social restoration. A cochlear implant can be a powerful tool for assimilation, for conforming with specific sets of behavioral norms, like hearing and speaking to have a conversation.

Now, the problem arises when those cultural norms threaten to diminish other equally rich and valuable ways of being in the world, such as communicating visually through sign language.

So, if I got a cochlear implant, I already knew I wasn't looking to be fixed. I didn't need to be fixed. I had grown up Deaf, with a wonderful family who gave me access to sign language. I was fine with the way I was. I knew a cochlear implant would not make me hearing. Like many other Deaf people, *I already felt whole.* So, here's what I wondered in 2009. I wondered if this piece of technology could still be a valuable tool for some situations. I wondered if it would be possible to get a cochlear implant and still be Deaf. Now, fast-forward to 2019, I never thought I would be here talking about this. I've had a cochlear implant for ten years now, and I have some news for you:

(**Via American Sign Language**) Yes, I'm still Deaf. In some ways, I'm more Deaf than I used to be. I haven't betrayed myself or my community. There are many different ways to be Deaf in the world. Having a cochlear implant introduced me to the strange, overwhelming, but also wondrous world of sounds. Many people are curious about this journey and what it was like. They want to know: how much can I hear now? How do I like it? I enjoy discussing the oddities of sound and hearing with other people. I really do. But here's another thing, which is often less recognized in the hearing world. I also like being able to *not* hear, to take my cochlear implant off, to communicate this way, with ASL. I like the attention to eye contact, space, and the body that I gain through being Deaf. I still see myself as a fundamentally Deaf person, even though I happen to hear and speak... sometimes, to some extent, in some situations.

I want to give you some examples of what I mean. First of all, my cochlear implant helped me to see how much I enjoyed silence. The first day I got my implant, I was thrilled that I could take it off. My deafness was still there. I would plunge into the chaotic world of sound for a few hours, and I'd feel awed (and sometimes annoyed) by the new spoken words I heard or the sounds of birds singing or dogs panting. But I also felt deep relief from knowing that I could still return to silence at the end of the day. I was especially grateful I could get a good night's sleep without being interrupted by some siren or a clap of thunder. How do you hearing people sleep at night, especially in a place like New York City? It's so loud. I really don't know how you do it.

My cochlear implant also helped me to see how spoken and auditory modes of communication can be useful tools, but not always, and not for everyone. We can all benefit from embracing more communicative flexibility. When I got my implant, I suddenly realized just how noisy most restaurants and public social spaces are. I couldn't hear myself think! My voice grew sore from shouting over other people. I started to observe how those other people didn't always hear each other, and they wouldn't admit it. Struggling through futile noise and sound felt like a waste.

My deafness gave me a valuable distance from these social norms. I already had other options to communicate. I could sign. I could gesture. I could write. I already knew how to use these tools. I saw how much of a gift that flexibility was, and I started wishing that more people could have access to it.

Finally, I realized that even if my cochlear implant was a useful tool for some situations, other technologies were equally useful for ensuring my right to communication. My implant helps for talking with other people in a quiet environment. It helps to alert me of many different beeps and buzzes and whistles in my world. But it's also shown me where my strengths already lie: in writing, seeing other people's faces, typing, and using my body to communicate.

Instead of trying to conform to auditory and verbal norms all the time, I've become more deliberate about embracing my strengths. The implant has given me fresh appreciation for other technologies like online messaging and Skype and FaceTime and captions and subtitles. None of these technologies cure deafness, or actually cure much of anything, but they're valuable *tools* for empowering many people. Sound or sight, or any other sensory channel, shouldn't be prerequisites for social inclusion. Rather, we can work toward integrating more of these different options into the world we live in.

(**Spoken**) Once upon a time, ten years ago, I worried that getting a cochlear implant would betray or erase my Deafness. Let me tell you, it hasn't. It's quite possible to be Deaf in the twenty-first century and have an implant. However, it's possible only when we think of Deaf people's experiences as fluid, flexible, nuanced, and even messy things. The fact that I have a cochlear implant still sometimes reinforces other people's binary ideas about "hearingness" or "deafness." It is in those spaces that I risk being erased.

I have conversations with new (hearing) acquaintances where it becomes tricky to explain how I can be Deaf and still hear, or how I can still hear some things, but still need accommodations, or how I can be speaking like I am right now and still not understand what they're saying. They become so confused about how I can (supposedly) hear them with my implant, without paying attention to how they can't sign like me.

(Via ASL) Sometimes I've had conversations with some Deaf people who worry that I seem "too hearing." I listen and speak. I have a cochlear implant. How Deaf am I, really? I tell those people I love my hearing friends and family, but I need deafness too. I need Deaf people to continue to exist in the world, in all their different forms. I need to recognize the very real privilege associated with sound and speech, and also work to empower more Deaf leadership and create more signing-accessible spaces.

(Spoken) My cochlear implant hasn't fixed my deafness. It's given me a new tool for navigating different communities and situations. Suggesting that I have been assimilated without realizing it, or that I must really be cured by now—both fail to recognize the complexity of my experience. I would like for us to see that, like virtually all other technologies, cochlear implants can be used by some people (sometimes) to advance their own flourishing in different ways. When we look at technologies as tools, not cures, we can consider more different options for communication. We can also pay more attention to the existing resourcefulness of deafness and disability.

I enjoy being someone who is Deaf but also hears some things, sometimes—and sometimes not at all. I contain multitudes, as we all do. And I'm looking forward to our conversation tonight about all of the ways we use technologies to take joy in each other's multiple different ways of communicating. Thank you.

(**Via ASL**) And now over to Teresa.

Teresa Blankmeyer Burke:

(**Signed in American Sign Language**): Hello. Hello, and good evening. It's so nice to see you all here tonight and to follow two wonderful presenters. Thank you both. The title of my presentation is called, "The Best for All of Us." And there's three parts, each of which has its own point or topic. I begin with "The Best of You."

I'd like to start with asking a question of the audience: How many of you are now or hope to become parents, please raise your hands. Anyone? About a third to a half of the audience. So, how many of you want the best for your child? You want them to have a good life, a flourishing life. Raise your hands again. [About a third to a half of the hands go up.] How do we fit technology into this discussion? We've seen these two presenters both talk about how technology can shape and support as well as help our lives. But I'd like to shift a little bit to talk about how technology can impact our lives before people are even born and how technology itself shapes our world and potential future.

Some of you might be familiar with the science fiction film called *Gattaca*. It is now part of the classic bioethics movie canon, and there is a famous scene with a genetic counselor who is talking with two potential parents. The counselors tell them that they can pick height; they can pick intelligence; they can choose how fast the child might run. They can pick a whole bunch of features about their potential child. And the mother was thinking, "Well, I don't know. I think I want to avoid illnesses, but I'm not sure how tall I might want the child to be." And the counselor says to the mother, "Your child will still be you but the best of you."

So, I guess most people who are themselves parents would like to pass along your genetic traits and characteristics that might benefit your child's life and give joy, but perhaps avoid passing along things that you would struggle with, things that you found frustrating. So, my question, then, is if you could use genetic technology to remove those negative traits—or traits that you perceive as negative—would you do so? If we think about the best of you, that depends on the context, the environment, right? Sometimes you have a genetic trait that expresses itself one way that perfectly fits a particular environment. But there's another time when that could be a mismatch, or a struggle, or the other way around. So, the environment—the context—is to a significant extent constituted by these technologies and how we deploy them. That's an important thing to consider when we're deciding to use technology that influences our next generations and whether our approach is open or closed to diversity in the world.

That brings me to point two about CRISPR (Clustered Regularly Interspaced Short Palindromic Repeats) technology. A year ago, in 2018, there was an announcement about the first use of this technology. A Chinese scientist named He Jiankui used CRISPR genome-editing technology to manipulate the genomes of two children prior to their birth in an attempt to make them immune to HIV infection. This was very controversial for many reasons, and I won't go into all of the details here, but I'd like to point out two things in particular that we need to know for our discussion.

It's a complicated technology but the underlying idea is easy to grasp. Suppose you have a phone, you know, and you're typing the word cat, C-A-T, but you really wanted to type the word cot, C-O-T, so you're able to do a quick, easy cut and paste. That's an oversimplification, but it's generally how the technology works.

If CRISPR is done on an early embryo, it doesn't only affect the person that embryo becomes; it also affects that person's descendants. So, we see this possibility for the threat and the elimination of our humanity, of elements of our human community.

Earlier this year, in July, a Russian scientist announced that he identified several deaf couples who were willing to consider the use of CRISPR gene-editing technology to ensure the birth of children who would be hearing, not deaf. My guess is that most hearing people would see this as being very positive, but it's not that easy or that simple of a decision. To see why the decision is more complicated than it might seem at first, it helps to appreciate a distinction that we philosophers make between necessary and sufficient conditions.

A necessary condition is something that is required for something to occur. Is hearing necessary for flourishing? Well, obviously there are people here on the stage tonight and beyond it who do not hear, but who have flourishing lives. And we all know people who do hear, but do not flourish. So we know that hearing is neither necessary nor "sufficient" for a flourishing life.

So maybe some of you are now saying to yourselves, "Yes, hearing is neither a necessary nor sufficient condition for flourishing, *but* . . . . Sometimes I hear my fellow philosophers make objections of this *yes, but* variety: "Well, yes, these people are exceptional, but their experience can't support any broader point." Or "yes, these people are flourishing, but their lives would be even better if they could hear." Or, "yes, these people are flourishing, but they miss out on a key human experience." "Well, yes, but look at the struggles they've had to deal with."

At the same time that we have some of these objections, I also have some more questions. How many of you would be willing to use a technology like CRISPR to have a child with a life that seems to fit your vision of the best flourishing life possible? Context is crucial. So, I'd like to change the frame. Now imagine a Deaf couple. And their lives are flourishing and very gratifying and rich as being a part of a beloved community and using a very powerful language. And they want their child to have the same thing, but they want a Deaf child. Can they use CRISPR to get the Deaf child that they desire? My sense, I might be incorrect, but my sense is that this topic, when I present it to a hearing audience, seems very unsettling; the idea of making a child deaf on purpose seems very controversial. But that sense of uneasiness is what many Deaf people experience when people talk about eliminating us from the world. CRISPR is a very powerful technology. How we decide to use it and if and when we decide to use it—all of these issues are very important.

One option is to use CRISPR; for many people, they think that perhaps it could be used to eliminate deafness and disability. And those people can then have good flourishing lives. Another view is maybe we see Deaf people who want to have their community legacy continue and don't want to use CRISPR for all situations because if they use CRISPR, they will lose some of the people within their own community and world.

Or perhaps we think about people with genetic disabilities and their experiences and their lives in the world with their genes and how they decide they don't want their children to experience the same kind of life, and they want to use CRISPR technology to change the type of life that their child might have. If we block CRISPR, if we stop that technology from developing, there could be serious repercussions. Some communities don't have the opportunity to have children. The Deaf couple that wanted Deaf children have a desire to use CRISPR to ensure they have a Deaf child like themselves, which supports their way of being in the world and flourishing. And that is a way to see the Deaf community survive.

I recognize that these options are all fraught with controversy. I'd like to add one last comment and perspective from a disabled bioethicist, Adrienne Asch. She wrote about *selective mentality*. The idea is that if we focus too much on one characteristic, one trait—deafness, for example, or sightedness or blindness—we fail to see the whole person, and thereby create a world that is ultimately worse for all of us. And so now we have this tension. We have the tension of acceptance versus control. And I invite us all to start this conversation about the sense of acceptance and the sense of control and the balance for using technology and accepting or rejecting technologies: how we can together create a world and an environment that supports all of us. Thank you. *And just imagine.*

Thank you, Rosemarie?

Rosemarie Garland-Thomson:

Thank you, Haben, Rachel, Teresa, Erik, the NEH, The Hastings Center, and all of you for coming. I'm delighted to be here on the podium with my three colleagues and good friends.

One question that people with disabilities often get asked goes something like this: "Would you rather be deaf or would you rather be hearing?" People often ask me some version of this question, like whether I'd like to have typical hands and arms instead of the unusual hands and arms that I actually have. My blind friend tells me that people frequently ask her if she'd rather be sighted or blind. Now, this kind of hypothetical offer of cure has always seemed really nonsensical to me, especially for those of us who have had our disabilities from birth or early on. Our disabilities can't simply be pried off of us. They are who we are. Perhaps the three of you would like to reflect a little bit on how questions or propositions such as this sit with you.

Haben Girma:

I've had that question many, many times. People ask, "Would you rather be blind or deaf?" Like anyone had that choice. Honestly, they're all cool. I've had an amazing life. I do love developing tools, developing my skills and talents. If someone offered me the ability to fly, if I could just spread my wings and go to California tomorrow, I'd love that skill. I'd take it. That would be an amazing gift. Until then, I'll take an airplane. That'd be helpful, but it's not necessary. You can flourish and thrive without flying.

Rachel Kolb:

(**Via ASL**): I can speak to that as well. When somebody asks me that question, "would I rather be hearing?" I would say, "I'd rather be myself." I don't have any other experience, from growing up and from my relationships with friends and family. My Deaf experience has made me who I am. And so that's why, if other people ask me something like that, it's like asking, "Would you rather be someone else other than yourself?" I can't separate who I am from my disability, from the experience of living in my body. We all have experiences of living in our bodies, in the world, and they're all unique. They make you who you are. Your interactions with people and with your environments are what make you who you are. And going through the world as a Deaf person isn't something I would give up just to fit in with a normative sense of what hearing people think is the way to live in the world.

Teresa Blankmeyer Burke:

(**Via ASL**): What I'm thinking about is how having so many different identities shapes my response to that question. For example, I'm Deaf. Yes, and I grew up hard of hearing, and I'm a woman. I'm straight and cisgender. And I'm also Arab American, and so it's all of those elements that become who I am; and I can't unplug one component, just pulling out the deaf part or pulling out the female part. All of these are interconnected and intersectional for my sense of identity. And they're all valuable parts of my life.

Rosemarie Garland-Thomson:

All three presenters this evening have told us how they use the designed and the built world in order to flourish. Rachel and Haben have explained the communication tools that they used to extend their bodies out into the world in order to connect with other people, both deaf people and hearing people. In this sense, people with disabilities are what Elizabeth Jackson calls "lifehackers." We take the given tools and the ways of doing things of the nondisabled majority, and we make them anew for ourselves. Now, all three of you have suggested that this opportunity for innovation and resourcefulness has benefited you in adapting to living in a world that's not built for us. I'd like to invite you—each of you—to give us a few more examples of how this capacity for resourcefulness and adaptability has benefited you or other people from our shared disability community.

Rachel Kolb:

(Via ASL): I'll start and respond to that. I would say my answer is probably familiar to a lot of the Deaf and signing people in this audience. Oftentimes in the hearing world, people think that speaking and hearing is the only way to communicate. But when I travel internationally, I meet strangers who will, of course, at first try to talk with me. And even if we don't know the same language, somehow, we can find a way of communicating, whether it's with gesture, our bodies, or facial expression. I'm able to connect with new people. And it's surprising. It's surprising to many of my hearing friends sometimes.

I remember a while ago I was traveling with a friend internationally, overseas, and we did not speak the local language, and we went into a shop to buy some sunscreen because it was a really hot, sunny day outside and we hadn't packed any. So, we went into the store and my hearing friend, in her hearing way, went to the woman who worked there and started to say, "Sunscreen, we need sunscreen." She tried writing it down in English. But again, mind you, this woman did not speak English. We were overseas. So, their language, for these two hearing people, was a barrier. I went up to the woman and did this: I gestured, rubbing sunscreen on my face. I gestured to the sun above and showed that it was very hot. My hearing friend was floored by how I had been able to traverse that barrier. It was a new option for communication she hadn't considered. That's something many people would call "Deaf gain," that ability to use our deafness to find new ways of overcoming obstacles and new ways of interacting through a more visual, tactile way to communicate. Do you want to add anything, Teresa?

Teresa Blankmeyer Burke:

(Via ASL): Yes, I would like to add a similar point about deaf gain. ASL is not my first language, and many of you who are signers might probably recognize this. When I arrived at Gallaudet University—which is a signing university, everyone signs to varying extents—I was trying to figure out how I can teach philosophy in sign language. And it occurred to me that what I needed to figure out is how we do philosophy in ASL. Maybe I'm not starting by borrowing from English per se, but how can I address my students and invite my colleagues into discussions about how we can do *Deaf philosophy*. And then we may be able to see what we can contribute to philosophical discussions in general, because it's not just about what we can figure out in terms of how we can accommodate the greater society, your hearing world, but how hearing society can also accommodate the Deaf community and what we have to contribute to one another.

Rosemarie Garland-Thomson:

Since we have a minute or two, I'll add something to my own question. Rachel Kolb and I work together. And one of the really interesting, I guess, "resourcefulness experiences" that have come out of working together is that we have—even though we both identify as people with disabilities—we have complementary and yet contrasting preferred modes of communication. I don't type (well, I kind of can type), but my preferred mode of communication is talking. Rachel's preferred mode of communication is typing, and in working together we have used technology in really interesting ways to discover delightful new languages, a kind of poetics that comes from my dictating, talking to my machine, and her inputting in her machine with her fingers. And it's been really interesting for us to learn or to develop this *new poetics*, really, in our communication together.

Rachel Kolb:

(**Via ASL**): Jumping off from there: learning how to think in a way that we don't normally think is another thing that's been instrumental for me. I don't talk to my phone. I don't dictate messages, but then I stop and think about talking to my phone and dictating. How would that work? I mean, obviously for you, you don't type emails. We're entering into each other's worlds and getting insight into each other's experiences; it's truly wonderful.

Teresa Blankmeyer Burke:

(**Via ASL**): And this is Teresa also adding a comment.[2] I think it's really interesting to think about how our very recent conversation of the four of us having and figuring out, okay, you know, Haben gave me the keyboard . . . and then Rachel was speaking . . . and I'm looking up at her speaking . . . and I'm also looking down and I'm typing; and I was just thinking, how, you know, it's one big benefit, I think, of the disability community: having this flexibility to see that we have a situation come up and we need to figure out how best to accommodate everyone. And we try something. And maybe if that doesn't work, we'll try something else. And then one more person joins in the conversation and we're incorporating them. Something that I really cherish and admire about our disability community is that flexibility. And I do wish that more people had this flexibility, this innate flexibility in our mainstream society. And I think that something that's really challenging is how to figure out how to share this attitude of having this flexibility in terms of communication, as well as open-mindedness in terms of being able to accommodate a range of experiences and ways of expression.

Rosemarie Garland-Thomson:

The last question for tonight: In modern liberal societies, parents have an obligation to provide their children with the sustenance and support that they need to flourish. As Teresa has suggested, modern medical science offers parents ways to shape their children according to the preferences that the parents have determined to be the most advantageous traits. Now what all three of you have suggested in your presentations is that what a typical parent might consider an advantage or a disadvantage has not determined your own flourishing. And I'd like to ask you to reflect a bit on this dilemma that modern parents face in the form of advice that you might have for parents as they make decisions about what they think will be their children's futures and their children's opportunities.

Teresa Blankmeyer Burke:

(Via ASL): Well, as a parent myself, I'm very hesitant to give advice, but I'm thinking about one kind of experience that I think is pretty common for most parents. When my first child was born, I remember having this dream as I stared into their eyes that they would do all of these kinds of things in the world that I loved, things that I appreciated. And then my child decides to love other things, and I'm trying to figure out how to be supportive of those interests, to learn from my child. And, at the same time, give them what they want and need with my sense of reasonable limits, with support, and with love. And now my children have grown. And I think something that I value the most about becoming a parent are those unexpected experiences: what I learned from my children and what I learned about myself from being a parent and how the relationship has really shaped both of us and how our environment has shaped those relationships. So, if I were to have advice, I would say it would be to be open to what life presents you with in terms of your experience of being a parent, because you never know what you get.

Haben Girma:

My biggest advice for parents is to learn alongside your kids. My parents thought, "Learning sign language is beautiful. We should learn sign language." They never got around to learning sign language. The same thing happened with braille. I've seen this in other families, too, where a disabled child is in a nondisabled family and has completely different experiences. It would really be cool if a family could learn alongside a child. So, if a child uses a wheelchair, understand wheelchairs. Become an expert in wheelchair use, alongside your child. If your child is deaf, learn sign language with them. Make it part of the whole family. Same thing with braille, other tools, and devices. Learn to use them together. By doing that, you can combat isolation and exclusion.

Rachel Kolb:

(**Via ASL**): One quick thing I'd add: I think there's a difference between the perception of learning new things and being a burden. Maybe think about it as an opportunity. Think about this as a positive advantage for the whole family that will really enrich the family's relationship. I think Teresa put it well when she talked about flexibility and open-mindedness and different ways of learning and interacting with one another. If parents want to be supportive of their children, they'll do that because it'll have a ripple effect. And if you start doing it with your family, it'll ripple out to the whole community. It won't just stay in that little nuclear family structure. It'll bleed throughout the community, and it will benefit everyone because we all are interdependent and have to support each other in our everyday lives.

2

Navigating

On Disability, Technology, and Experiencing the World

Yomi Sachiko Young, Rod Michalko, and Kim Q. Hall

Liz Bowen:

Welcome, everyone. Good afternoon. This is "Navigating: On Disability Technology and Experiencing the World." My name's Liz Bowen, I am the Rice Family Postdoctoral Fellow at the Hastings Center, and I am one of the co-organizers of this event.

Erik Parens:

Thanks very much, Liz, for all your contributions to making this event happen, and thanks to all of you for joining us. The purpose of this series is to broadcast and to explore one fundamental theme, which is that *people can flourish in all sorts of bodies*. To flourish, in our understanding, means to exercise the capacities we were born with in pursuit of the goals we find meaningful. None of us needs a different body to flourish. We need different, more supportive environments. I should say that no one has articulated our theme more powerfully than Rosemarie Garland-Thomson, who is a co-organizer of this event, a senior advisor to and fellow of The Hastings Center, and, as many of you know, a pioneering disability scholar. I should also mention that we at The Hastings Center view this series as an important part of our fiftieth anniversary celebration.

Because the term "bioethics" has many connotations, I want to say something about what it means at The Hastings Center. Since its inception, many of us have thought critically about the meanings of many familiar medical technologies, for example, those monitors that are above patients' hospital beds. The concern is that in drawing doctors' attention to a single feature of how a patient's body is functioning, such technologies can take doctors' attention away from the patient as a whole person. Bioethicists at Hastings have also been concerned that reproductive technologies like prenatal genetic testing are being used to ensure that only people with certain sorts of bodies will be welcomed into the human community. And we've been concerned that medical professionals sometimes foist onto people with atypical bodies some very old-fashioned technologies, like leg braces, with the intention of fixing people who don't need any fixing at all. So, we at Hastings have often emphasized that such technologies have been integral parts of systems that can thwart the flourishing of many people and in particular, disabled people. In developing that line of critique, we have not always given equal attention to the myriad ways that people in general and people with disabilities in particular use technologies to promote their flourishing.

To our credit, when we conceived of this series, we said that we wanted to explore the fact that technologies can be used both to thwart and to promote flourishing. We were using the term "technology" as a hook to get to our fundamental theme: that people can flourish in all sorts of bodies. Today, however, it is, frankly, not crystal clear to me that the term "technology" is all that great a hook for getting at our theme. But a beautiful thing about being in conversation, as we are today, is that we have the option of revising our thinking. Indeed, the question of the usefulness of the term "technology" might come up today in the panel discussion that

Rosemarie Garland-Thomson will moderate with our speakers, or it might come up in the conversation between all of you in the audience and our speakers that Joel Michael Reynolds will moderate. Joel was the inaugural Rice Family Postdoctoral Fellow at The Hastings Center, and he is the codirector of this series. He's also a philosopher, bioethicist, and disability studies scholar who is now at Georgetown University.

The term "activity" is another hook we have used to get at our fundamental theme. Each of our six events is linked to an activity that can be crucial for some person's flourishing, and each of our speakers today will consider the activity of navigating.

Our first speaker is Yomi Sachiko Young. Yomi is a healthcare professional, a freelance journalist, and disability justice activist who will explain the fundamental importance of being able to choose a technology that fits with one's sense of oneself and allows one the ability to navigate freely. Yomi, over to you.

Yomi Sachiko Young:

Thank you, Erik, and "Hi" everyone! I'm Yomi Sachiko Young joining from the land of smoke and fire, otherwise known as Northern California. I am an African American woman with dark, curly, shoulder-length hair and glasses. I am a little person. I'm sitting in a power wheelchair with a bookcase behind me. I'm excited to be here, and I appreciate The Hastings Center for inviting me into this conversation on navigating.

The story I chose today is very tender to me. I've not spoken about it much and feel nervous to share it, but here it is. I was my best self at nine years old: happy, witty, and confident. I truly liked who I was. I had hit a stride in fourth grade. I mastered long division, was reading and writing above eighth-grade level, had beautiful penmanship, and performed at the top of my class. Adding to my confidence, I was cute and popular! There is a picture of me on the bookshelf over my left shoulder. That's me at nine years old, in the fourth grade. It's black and white; I have pigtails and bangs; I'm smiling and wearing a velour shirt because this was 1981 or so and that was the fashion.

So, at that age, peers gravitated to me. I was outgoing and a natural leader who tried to always make others feel included. At school, I was often paired with shy kids, my task being to help draw them out. Or I was paired as a study buddy with someone needing extra help in a subject where I excelled. This latter gift is how I straddled two different realities at my elementary school, and this led to an unfortunate incident that would shape so much of my disability identity. My fourth grade teacher thought I needed more intellectual rigor and arranged for me to quasi-mainstream into a sixth grade Science and Math class. Mainstreaming, if you're unfamiliar with the term, is the process of transitioning disabled kids from segregated educational settings into public schools with able-bodied kids. Now, I very much liked my school, my classmates, and especially my teacher. But to be honest, the experience of being bussed twenty minutes away while friends on my block walked together to the neighborhood school built up a longing inside me.

I wanted to be with them. Going to a different school excluded me from a huge part of their world and the divide was becoming harder to overlook. For instance, when they laughed about the antics in Mrs. So-and-so's homeroom, I couldn't follow the joke. After school, when a gaggle of kids charged into the bodega for ice cream or candy, or the local pizzeria to play video games, I was never included, because I wasn't with them. I knew nothing of the games they invented at recess. I knew nothing of team sports or how to navigate a cafeteria. I'm sorry. . . . What exactly happens in a lunchroom?

You see, in my special education school, we took our meals in the classroom. Except for physical therapy or trips to the bathroom, we rarely left our classroom or one another. It seemed we were too precious for recess, too fragile to jockey in hallways, too fussed over to rip and run after school.

Being in special education for me meant being *segregated*, virtually invisible to anyone outside our walls. So, this chance my teacher was giving me to leave my cloistered environment and dwell in a rarefied space with able-bodied children felt like a golden ticket.

The school I attended was on the first floor of a multistory building. The upper floors were occupied by a public elementary school with hundreds of kids we could glimpse, but never interact with. So, each week, I left my community on the first floor and rode an elevator up to the public school.

Of course, I was initially treated as a freak. Kids stared and giggled, but over time, we all got used to me being in the space. Soon I was paired with a boy who needed support with math and we became great friends. I don't remember his name, but I remember his kindness, his bright smile, and the happiness I felt when the elevator doors would open and he would be waiting there to escort me to class. We had so much fun together.

A few months into the school year, this perfect friend asked if I wanted to go to a movie over school break. Calm down; it was not a date. We were nine years old. But it *was* a big deal.

Meeting up for activities outside of school was a social and developmental milestone I was missing out on. Some of the details of this movie caper are fuzzy, but this is what I remember: it somehow worked out that his big brother and my big sister would escort us to a matinee. And I felt like these teenagers must have hijacked the encounter because they each ended up inviting an extra friend, but whatever.

Movie day arrived, and my mom left money for tickets, snacks, and cab fare. This last detail is critical. You see, had we taken the bus, I wouldn't be able to go to the movies in my wheelchair, clunky and rigid and impossible to haul on the bus or subway as it was. This was 1981 in the Bronx, New York, a full decade before the

Americans with Disabilities Act made public transportation accessible. But with cab fare, there was no need to leave my chair behind. With a little muscle, my wheelchair could be folded up and placed in the trunk of a car.

But for reasons still mysterious to me, someone made the decision not to take my wheelchair. It was decided that I would go to the movies in a stroller.

So now would be a good time to mention that for most of my early childhood I had two modes of mobility. The wheelchair, which I used primarily at school and around my neighborhood, and a lightweight toddler stroller.

Navigating New York City (NYC), and, really, anywhere as a pedestrian was much easier to do with me in a stroller. Unlike my wheelchair, one person could pick me up and collapse the stroller in seconds. We could then run up subway steps or hop on a bus or even hail a cab very quickly. The stroller weighed next to nothing.

In the NYC of my childhood, a toddler stroller was my family's most convenient piece of adaptive technology because it allowed for greater access and movement around the city. But the stroller also changed how I showed up in the world.

Tucked down so low to the ground as I was in a stroller, everything about me became obscured. My age, what grade I was in, even the fact of my disability. Unless I opened my mouth to speak, strangers could easily take me for a toddler or a child of maybe three to five years old.

Let me say, this worked brilliantly at amusement parks that let toddlers and little kids in for free, but I don't think this was the motivating factor for the person in my family accompanying me to the movies that day. It was the carrying me down the apartment stairs to the cab, the breaking my wheelchair apart for transport, the putting it together again at the movie theater, and then repeating the whole rigamarole for the return trip home. I acknowledge this was a hassle. And again, I have blocked out some details of what occurred next and no one in my family remembers it quite this way. But it didn't happen to them. Emotion imprints memory, and here's the way I experienced these events:

Someone said, "We're just going to take your stroller, okay?"

"Um, no," I protested. "I will not go to the movies in a baby stroller."

"But you've done it before!"

"That was before. This is today. Different stakes." I threw an epic fit; my mother was called at work to mediate. I wanted her to force these teenagers to bring my bloody wheelchair!

Someone, maybe my mother but possibly my sibling said, "If he's really your friend, Yomi, it won't matter how you show up!"

They were right, technically, and I had no counterargument. Again, I was nine and in the throes of a meltdown. I clearly recall not wanting to go anymore but being made to go anyway. I remember feeling so sick in the cab. I remember hot tears running down my face. I remember praying we would crash. Dramatic, I know. But, for me, seeing a school friend out in the real world for the very first time was a big deal as is. Must we make it awkward, too?

I feared my friend's reaction to seeing his smart school chum stripped of mobility, autonomy, and independence, effectively infantilized. Seeing me so out of context. Would it be too much? Indeed, it was.

I remember this next painful sequence in slow motion.

That sweet boy dancing nervously in front of the ticket booth and rushing to greet the cab when we pulled up to the curb. My sister emerges first, pretty and smiling. She whips out the stroller. My friend looks confused. Then she lifts me from the backseat, plops me into the stroller, and straps me in like a baby.

My poor friend looks on, horrified. The older boys with him look befuddled, unsure who has shown up. Certainly not the vibrant schoolgirl he's been talking so much about.

The moment turns rancid with my mortification. My sister, ever my champion and my shield, breaks the terrible moment by striding up to the ticket counter, doing her best to lighten the air. But my friend looked away, and I did too. We did not talk the rest of the day. And back at school things shifted. We stopped studying together. We stopped looking at each other. We stopped being friends.

Like I said earlier, I've hardly spoken of this to anyone, but it has stayed with me, and I have spent forty-some years trying to get over it, to make meaning of it.

My wheelchair, more than any piece of assistive technology, is *the thing I will fight for* because there are real and unforgiving consequences for disabled folks when we are denied technology of our own choosing. The wrong technology can inflict physical pain, lead to secondary impairments, or imprint deep emotional scars. When I choose for myself, I source technology that is as much about maximizing my function as about making the right statement of who I am.

My chair is how I first get read when I show up in any space. I fill in the rest, of course, but my chair gives much important information at the start. Thank you.

Erik Parens:

Thank you, Yomi, for such a wonderful talk. I'd like to now introduce Rod Michalko. Rod is a sociologist, memoirist, and disability studies theorist who lives in Toronto and is retired from teaching at University of Toronto.

Rod Michalko:

Thank you. First of all, I'd like to say: Yomi, that was a beautiful talk, and I'm going have to remind myself never to follow her again. She's a tough act to follow!

I'm a blind white guy and I'm, I think, about average build. I'm not sure about that. I think I have long, kind of wavy hair and I'm wearing dark glasses that are blue and hopefully match my purple t-shirt. If not, I'm going to blame my partner Tanya for that. (I'm kidding about that.) I'm sitting at home. There's a bookcase behind me. I'm going to do my talk on a piece of technology that's so dated that I'm sure many of you don't even know the term. It's called a Dictaphone, and on this Dictaphone is a tape of what I'm about to say. And I'm going to repeat it with this ear-thing in. So, I'm going to start that, and please indulge me for your time if I mess up. Thank you, and by the way, welcome, everybody. I'm glad you're all here.

The freedom of movement is something many people take for granted. Some have the freedom to move from one country to another, from one region to another. Some move freely between careers and jobs; and many have the freedom of bodily movement, the freedom to sit, to stand, to walk, and to run. The freedom to move freely in a city such as New York or Toronto, where I live. The freedom to negotiate a flight of stairs, escalators, elevators. The freedom to drive cars, take public transit, and the freedom to negotiate the rest of the environment, built especially for those who take the freedom of movement for granted.

There are some, however, perhaps even many, whose freedom of movement is restricted beyond any typical limitation and for whom free movement is not taken for granted. I am speaking here of disabled people. We negotiate an environment, one that is not built for us, and we do so daily. I want to talk about the unique world my blindness gives me and how my late guide dog Smokie and I moved freely with my blindness in this world.

First thing I want to say about this blind gig is that, while it does impose some limits on my freedom to move, it is sight and the way it organizes the environment that hits my freedom to move and hits it hard. The material and the virtual worlds are built by and for those who see. This is the world I negotiate and have negotiated all of my blind life.

Movement in the world, free or not, is almost always accompanied by technology. Whether walking with the technology of footwear, traveling in airplanes or trains, whether moving in wheelchairs, with white canes or with guide dogs, whether negotiating in the virtual world with nimble fingers on a keyboard, and quick eyes on a screen, or with software that imitates such movements, poorly as they do, in whatever way we move, we move with technology at our side.

For many years I moved with, literally at my side, my guide dog Smokie. He didn't so much move me through the world as he moved me *in the world* and *in blindness* as he accompanied me in my movement. Although he did guide me through the world, I experienced it more as a liberation, as being free to move. This was my experience with Smokie in the beginning of our life together. Soon though, I began to realize that it wasn't only that Smokie accompanied me. We accompanied one another, blind man and dog moving together, negotiating a world not strictly ours. The world in which Smokie and I moved was a sighted world, one where people looked and saw. It was a human world, one where people moved, so many and so freely, on two legs, and in a world they typically experienced from a point much higher than the place from which Smokie viewed the world.

It was a sighted world, a human world. There were blind people and dogs in that world of course, but it wasn't a blind world nor a dog world. And it was in *this* world that Smokie and I moved.

We were not complete strangers to the world, however. We had experience with the world, estranged as we were from it. Smokie was a dog, an animal. At the same time though, he was a guide dog, highly trained, intelligent, and aware. Moreover, like other dogs in our culture, Smokie was domesticated. The world of humans was his home, even though Smokie himself wasn't human. With his high level of training, he was not only accepted in the world of humans, he was also understood as a useful and thus valuable member of that world, assisting me, a blind person, in navigating a world fashioned for and by sight.

I, in contrast, am human—and not in the way Smokie was an animal. There is something unnatural about my humanness. It is "natural" for humans to see; I don't. And therein lies my "unnatural" human status. Whereas Smokie represents domesticated nature, I represent the unnatural nature of the human, with eyes *gone wrong*. The estranged familiarity that Smokie and I *were* was the fertile ground for experiencing the world stripped of its taken-for-granted character.

Our life together presented us with the unusual opportunity to see some of the ways our world is put together, ways that are as invisible as sight itself. Smokie not only showed me ways of negotiating the world, but he also gave me a glimpse of that world from an entirely different viewpoint, a viewpoint that revealed some of the invisible features of the sighted world. The most crucial thing Smokie gave me was a further reach into the world. He also firmed up my contact with it, a contact that permitted further reach. Until then, I had three points of contact: my two feet and the artificial contact of my white cane. Smokie gave me six: my two feet and his four paws, none of which were artificial. My reach into the world was now extended by the length of his body and by the speed and assured grace of his movement. I didn't so much follow Smokie as I moved with him through the world, negotiating it with a habitual rhythm that came eerily close to moving confidently and with, most surprisingly, joy.

There were, of course, many close calls Smokie and I had as we moved, such as the time that he suddenly cut across my body and moved me away from a speeding car running a red light. There were also many fun times, such as the time we visited a summer fair in rural Nova Scotia. He loved animals and walking through one of the barns housing farm animals proved to be Smokie's favorite time. It wasn't easy to encourage him out of there, and when I was finally successful, we continued our tour of the fairgrounds. Smokie's intricate movements around the unfamiliar grounds soon were too much for me, and I allowed Smokie to show me the fairgrounds in the way that he chose. I got caught up in Smokie's flow, clearly his intention since, in a few minutes, we were back at the barn.

Smokie did free my blindness into the world even in the midst of the not-so-freeing stereotypes and often bizarre representations of blindness and of guide-dog teams our culture offered as we moved. But as Smokie and I moved in this strange and unfamiliar world, it released yet another freedom: the freedom to belong in that world and to belong on our terms. Smokie did help me negotiate this world, but he made it clear the world we were moving in and through was *our world*. We belonged there. And we belonged as blind and sighted, moving and living together as human and animal, forming the basis of this strange yet familiar life.

With my left hand on Smokie's harness and a simple, "Forward, Smokie," we entered the places and spaces, the sounds, the touches, and the smells that were our world. We were one of those places and spaces, one of those sounds, touches, and smells. We were not, though, merely one more of "them," seen with the banal gaze of difference. Instead, we were distinct. We were the sight of blindness, not as the banality of difference, but as the richness of distinction. And never before had I moved through the world where sight did not have the right of way.

"Forward, Smokie." And then . . . movement, speed, grace. The world opened before us as Smokie and I, and our world, elegantly entered it.

Thank you.

Erik Parens:

Rod, thank you so much for another wonderful talk. Kim Q. Hall, our third speaker, is currently a philosophy professor and scholar of gender, women's, and sexuality studies at Appalachian State

University in Boone, North Carolina. (Kim Q. Hall is now based at the University of Alberta in Edmonton, Alberta, Canada.) Over to you, Kim!

Kim Q. Hall:

Thanks, Erik. And thanks, everyone, for being here and thanks again, Yomi and Rod, for these wonderful talks.

My walk has always been a problem, or I should say that my walk has always made me a problem. I was born with what in my life has often been referred to as a malformed hip joint. More specifically, I was born with a shortened acetabulum, which means that my hip socket did not completely curl around my femoral head on my left side. It was a case, one might say, of arrested hip development. Not enough hip, not hip enough. My so-called birth defect was diagnosed during a routine pediatric exam meant to check for such anomalies. When the pediatrician bent my knees toward my chest and then rolled them outward, he heard the telltale sound of my left femur popping out of joint, and when my mother changed my diapers, my left leg would fly off at an awkward angle. I have no memory of what my hip popping out of joint felt like. However, I do have memories of treatment, of being wheeled into surgery, being casted and braced, having my cast changed when I outgrew it, regular follow-up appointments with the orthopedic surgeon, and the dreaded trip to the shoe store where I was never permitted to get the shoes I wanted—for orthopedic *and* gendered reasons.

I was nearly two when I had surgery on my left hip. This was followed by three months in a body cast, coupled with a brace that consisted of a metal bar between two shoes that kept my feet fixed in position, pointing outward. All of this meant that my walking was delayed. One of my uncles attached four wheels to a piece of plywood so that I could roll around the house. My earliest ambulation in the world was headfirst, on my stomach. My mom says I was hard to catch. By first grade, I was no longer braced at night, but I still had to go to the orthopedic clinic, where I was X-rayed and where I was required to walk up and down the hallway in front of the diagnostic gaze of the orthopedist and my mother. The result? The orthopedic conclusion was that I was fixed, cured, if you will. The result from my perspective: I walk, but with a difference. In my remarks today, I want to reflect on why and how this difference matters.

My focus is not on whether technological intervention is good or bad. Technology can be informed by an ableist commitment to disability elimination, and it can be used in creative, resistant ways for disability flourishing. But the effects of technology can also exceed these aims, creating zones of embodied being in the world at the edges of ability and disability.

Within ableist contexts, what is either abled or disabled? A technological intervention like surgery moves one from abnormal to normal, from disability to ability. How might we understand navigation at the edges of these categories? In an effort to think about some of the issues raised by this question, I focus on two points. First, how my gait troubles ableist assumptions about the distinction between ability and disability, and second, how we might think about flourishing *between* ability and disability.

First, *gait*. I have what many characterize as a limp, though it is a limp that also embodies a swagger. I have walked under the diagnostic gaze of doctors, and I have been periodically chastised for walking like my father and like a truck driver. These accusations signal that my gait defies both abled and gendered expectations. I have a limping swagger, or a swaggering limp. Either way, my gait exceeds the bounds of the normal. From an ableist perspective, the surgery, bracing, et cetera, were successful because they fixed an impairment that would have prevented walking. That said, from a perspective that I call "queer and crip," these technological interventions did not completely erase my body's difference. My gait bears the trace of disability experience, situating me between ability and disability in ways that call into question ordinary assumptions about those categories and their relationship.

In an ableist society, the aim of curative technologies is disability elimination. The orthopedic technological interventions I experienced aimed to normalize my body to make it possible for me to navigate the world by walking. Still, my limping, swaggering gait violates gendered, heteronormative, and ableist expectations of how a body like mine is supposed to move through the world. While my gait might not count within narrow legal and medicalized understandings of disability, it is shaped by disability experience. Walking does not make me anonymous for reasons to do with gender and disability. It's not uncommon to encounter a stranger's stare that first goes to my foot and leg and then takes in the rest of me. Sometimes the starer just stares. In limping, swaggering along, I confess that it's difficult, if not impossible, for me to know whether the stare is initially directed at my limp, or my gender nonconforming swagger. But both converge to shape how I navigate the world between ability and disability.

Second, *flourishing between disability and ability*. I use the phrase "queer crip" to describe this way of navigating the world, drawing on Nancy Mairs's explanation of why she prefers to identify as crippled rather than disabled. She writes, "as a cripple, I swagger."[1] Like the word "queer," "cripple" has a history of being weaponized against a marginalized group singled out by the term. And like "queer," "crip," a shortened form of "cripple," has been reclaimed by many to describe experiences that aren't typically associated with disability and to name a politics of proud, spectacular defiance of pressures to assimilate to exclusionary norms. Queer and crip call for a more expansive understanding of gender, sexuality, ability, and disability, attuned to experiences that defy conventional assumptions about who is included in or excluded from a category like disability. An experience of being disabled at birth and then subjected to medical interventions aimed at normalizing the body by erasing disability is not what most people have in mind when they think of disability experience. Within conventional understandings of disability, my experience might be categorized as an experience of cure.

Nonetheless, in limping one stands out, and one's navigation is often interrupted by questions like "What's wrong?" and "What happened?" and "What did you do to yourself?" Such questions communicate that one doesn't belong. To limp is to fail to meet expectations of fluid motion, a monstrous occupation of space. When one has been categorized as cured, the limping gait defies expectations of how abled, normal bodies move. "But you had surgery, and you were able to play sports? Why are you limping?"

To swagger is also to defiantly move through space. A swagger is an embodied assertion of self that is unconcerned with what others might think. When it's part of one's gender nonconforming ways in the world, a swagger flouts gendered expectations by asserting one's presence in the world, predicated on one's shame, misery, or nonexistence. And so, in characterizing my gait as queer crip navigation, I aim to reframe disability and ability beyond the framework of diagnosis and cure and to understand how heteronormativity, ableism, and other forms of oppression work together to normalize bodyminds. As queer crips know in our bones and joints, orientations toward the normal won't cure what ails us or create possibilities for flourishing.

Following the concept of "deaf gain" in deaf studies, the term "disability gain" has been used to describe disability as a source of knowledge about and creative being in the world. Disability gain defies ableist assumptions of disability as a lack of ability, or disabled people as objects rather than subjects of knowledge. Perhaps what I am thinking about here might be called "crip gain," a perspective between ability and disability that troubles the boundaries of both. What can be gained from understanding experiences of childhood medical interventions not as eliminating or curing disability, but instead as situating one between disability and ability in ways that don't make one disabled in a legal or medical sense but nonetheless positioned as queer crip? I suggest that such queer crip navigations offer a perspective of how various forms of oppression work together to impede or enable navigation in the world and forge paths of aspirational solidarity with others who, for various reasons, are denied free movement in the world. Rather than aim for a fixed destination, queer crip navigations open possibilities for flourishing at the edges of normalizing conceptions of identity and belonging, thus suggesting another way to be.

Rosemarie Garland-Thomson:

Thank you very much to everyone who contributed to this really terrific event: the NEH, The Hastings Center, Joel, Erik, Liz, the support team, and most of all my fellow panelists, my colleagues, my friends, and my fellow travelers who have spoken. I am joining you today via Zoom from my home office in San Francisco, and I wanted to tell you a little bit about who I am. I am a senior woman educator with silver hair that's a lot longer than it used to be and pale skin that's a lot paler than usual. The technologies that I'm using here today include my glasses and the machines and applications that I need to use to be with you here today and to participate because I don't type.

I have a couple of questions that I want to present to our team of speakers, and these questions recapitulate in some ways what the speakers have thematized in their work and what they've said.

So, question one: each of you has offered a story about an event that shaped your *disability identity*. Those are the words that Yomi uses in talking about our stories. Each of your stories shows the ways that you get around in the world: our technology, and how we use that technology . . . how that technology—and I'm quoting Yomi again here—makes a statement of *who we are*. Technology such as wheelchairs, guide dogs, braces, and canes, are often understood as aides that compensate for what we can't do, or for some inadequacy the world seems to think we have. Your stories today show us how we use our technologies very intentionally to live in a world not built for us, as Rod tells us. We use technology to move from a segregated world that excludes people with disabilities to one where we can access opportunities such as education, employment, economic security, and housing, to enter into a world where we have what Rod calls "freedom of movement."

I'd like to ask the panelists to give us a few more examples of how you intentionally use the technology that you need to access the kind of resources that enable you to flourish as people with disabilities—as people with disabilities, rather than people who are trying to become nondisabled.

Yomi Sachiko Young:

Regarding the last part of your question about flourishing and being present as a person with a disability versus trying to not be disabled, I would say that right around maybe a few years after that period in the story that I told, I stopped participating in physical therapy. I stopped trying to use crutches and walkers. I was using those both to gain strength and mobility, and because it seemed important to people and to the medical community and to my family that I learn to walk. But the truth is, with my disability, which is osteogenesis imperfecta—I have brittle bones and I'm a very small person—it was quite unsafe for me to be walking, to go to school with a walker or crutches because I broke so easily. I could be walking or trying to exercise or ride on a tricycle. I could be doing nothing and get injured. I could sneeze and break a bone. In fact, *my wheelchair became protective.*

I use my wheelchair as an exoskeleton to move through the world, and I have just given up on some of those other types of devices and aids because I don't aspire to walk, ever. It is not safe for me to be a walking person in this world. I don't care to do it.

I don't know if that gets to every aspect of your question, but it did resonate when you talked about showing up as disabled, which for me is a personal identity. It is also a political identity and a point of pride, and when it comes to trying to approximate able-bodiedness, I have no interest.

Rosemarie Garland-Thomson:

Thanks. Kim, or Rod, did you want to say something about this question or follow up on what Yomi has said?

Kim Q. Hall:

Yes, just in terms of thinking about that question for me, I'm not somebody who has disability as an identity at present, but I was born disabled. And it's interesting to me in relation to conversations about disability in which folks often think about how disability is in the future, and is, of course, always a possibility. And yet it is part of my past, and it has shaped my habituation and embodied way of being in the world and how I think about myself and how I think about relations with others. So, I think about myself as *situated between* ability and disability.

But in terms of technology, I think about the square piece of plywood with wheels on it that my uncle made. That's something I loved throughout my childhood; it enabled me to get around quickly and to run away from people by rolling really fast out of the reach of adults . . . much faster than if I crawled or something like that, which I couldn't do. But, in terms of thinking about limping, swaggering, and technology that has been really important for me, I think shoes are incredibly important, both for gendered reasons and for supportive reasons. Not being able to choose the shoes I wanted was a part of my gender identity that was rendered invisible in that moment, which was also about disability. But, for me, part of walking or navigating in the world is also about doing so in ways that defy gendered and abled expectations of embodiment.

Rosemarie Garland-Thomson:

That's great. Rod did you want to address this particular question?

Rod Michalko:

Sure, thank you. I think there's one small point I'd like to make. While I think it's true that all of us who understand ourselves as disabled do use certain kinds of technology as a way to gain access to the world of economics and housing, et cetera—and that's hugely important—but as Yomi said, I view my blindness as political. It's that kind of identity. Technology for me is also about *how I bring blindness into the world* in a way that's different from the typical, sighted way of understanding it as a deficit of eyesight and as a mere difference. Rather than that, I find ways—and I have done this all my blind life—of bringing blindness as a distinction, a distinct way of being and bringing *that* into the world. Viewing technology not only as a way to access your world, but to bring my world *into your world* in a way that's distinct from how you have it.

Rosemarie Garland-Thomson:

Thank you, Rod. Rod and I have been friends a long time, and I love the way you talk about having *a blind life*. I find that very poetic. I'm an English teacher, and I love poetry and literature, so it's particularly important for me to be able to be involved in and hear your stories today, so thank you. I'm going to another question. In the stories you shared with us today about flourishing as people with disabilities, all three of you have used words that describe your lives and yourselves, which might be surprising words to people who do not know too many disabled people well.

Yomi spoke of having power. Rod spoke of experiencing grace and joy as a blind man. Kim spoke of her swagger not as a defect, but as a gain.

Can you tell us more about the benefits you've experienced in your life by living in a way that many people, really, society in general often understands not as power or gain or joy, but as deficit or defect?

Rod Michalko:

I'll start. Yeah, this is difficult. While I think Kim is right in that there's a certain gain with disability—in some sense, there's a kind of a gain with most ways of being in the world—I think rather than benefit or gain, one way I often think of my blindness is that the world lets me know that blindness is clearly something others don't want to have ... and that, sometimes, depending on my mood and during COVID-19 times, that's not really that great.

But my blindness has given me the opportunity to realize that *eyesight is the furthest thing from natural as possible*. You need to get a sense somehow, show one another that you can see. In a way, it's beautiful to "watch" from a blind point of view because sighted people are so busy demonstrating to one another that they can see that sometimes it's humorous. Other times, it's a little sad.

Nonetheless, it's really, really interesting and a lot of fun and joy to move in a world, particularly with my late guide dog Smokie, and talk to him as I move about and pretend that he actually answers back.

It's fascinating. One little example that I have is looking toward people when you are talking, something I can really imitate well.

It's interesting how well I can imitate seeing, and sight. Sometimes when I'm sitting in a place where nobody knows me, I'm taken for sighted, and I just love how the perceived accuracy of sight can be that tricky. I love tricking sighted people.

Rosemarie Garland-Thomson:

That's great. Yomi, Kim? Did you want to comment on joy, gain, power?

Kim Q. Hall:

I can comment on joy, I think. It's no fun, in some ways, not to be anonymous, having to be stopped and having your gait commented upon by whomever one might encounter while you're trying to go from one place to another sometimes. At the same time, I think joy has to do with a sense of living in ways that create new ways to be. I think there's navigation that is about forging a path of new ways of living and relating to others that I've found that incredibly joyful as a queer person.

Joel Michael Reynolds:

It's time to take questions from the audience, and I'd like to start with the following: each of the three speakers' presentations takes up, in different ways, the problem of ableism. Although "ableism" is a concept increasingly discussed in international media and other public spaces, it is not as well understood as related terms like "sexism" and "racism" are. Can you talk about what ableism means to you and why combatting it matters?

Kim Q. Hall:

That's a really important question. Ableism is the systematic and institutionalized normalization and naturalization of abled-bodied-mindedness, in the sense that being abled-bodied, having a certain appearance and way of moving through the world, is something taken as natural. Lots of people have written about this in disability studies, like Robert McRuer. In terms of my own thinking about ableism, I'm interested in how it both informs and is informed by other systems of oppression. One of the things Robert McRuer talks about is *compulsory* able-bodiedness and *compulsory* able-mindedness—the fact that there's an *imperative* to fit into these norms of embodiment and movement in the world.[2]

And I think what's so important about that is, first of all, no one really fully embodies these norms. Most of us in some sense fail to embody the norm, but its exclusionary force is quite harmful. It informs all kinds of efforts to normalize the body, whether through medical interventions or surgical "corrections." It also informs violence that people can encounter in the world. So, I think those institutionalized pressures to be normal are basically a part of what it is that informs and creates ableism.

Rod Michalko:

I think Kim was really good with her comments. Also, one of the things at play here: it's a systemic problem, really, that doesn't belong to disabled people, incidentally. It's related, of course, as Kim said, to racism and sexism and various kinds of systemic discrimination and exclusion. It does often lead to violence.

When people speak of various types of oppressions, like ableism, sexism, and racism, it's often accompanied with a "but not me." This idea of, "it's the system, not me," is sometimes one of the issues. It's interesting with disability, in my case blindness, how an ableist perspective is a sighted community speaking and thinking as though they understand blindness in some kind of complete way. First, there's the thought that it's an absence of sight, that is, an absence of who they are; and, second, that the person living with blindness would rather have what they have. There's that sense of "you'd rather be me, but you're not."

Then there's that ableist version of gain, which we spoke of, that we have somehow rather naturally compensated for our loss. In my case, loss of sight. Well, I hear better and smell better.

Often, people in a group will say things like "you will appreciate this, having better hearing." Then I'll say, "Pardon?" and often they'll either get it or not. So often there is ableist stuff that is informed by, to use Kim's terms, a more systemic ableist oppression.

Joel Michael Reynolds:

That's really powerful. And one of the things that I hear in both of your comments is the way in which one effect of ableism is to create what you could call ableist common sense. Right? The idea that leads to comments like "of course I'd like to be able to see and not be blind."

This kind of fundamental, default assumption that it's easy for able-bodied people to have, that being able-bodied in X, Y, or Z ways, is certainly better and desired. This ties back directly with Kim's citation of Robert McRuer's notion of compulsory able-bodiedness—an *imperative*, I think is the word you used, Kim, a command that operates often, not necessarily on a reflective level, but that operates in the background of people's assumptions about the world and how it should be.

Here is another question from the audience: How do you think the medical field should change in order to have a better response to and relationship with people with disability and disability communities? And the person who wrote this question then further specified, How do you think *your* specific interaction with it could have been better?

Yomi Sachiko Young:

I'll go first. I work in healthcare and so I have the opportunity to see the field from another view—both working in healthcare but also being a subject and participant my whole life within the medical model.

For me, when it comes to disability and impairment, we need to be preparing people and addressing function. For example, it would have been much better to prepare me to be an adult and function in the world as it is *rather than try to fix me* and try to make minor in-roads in an ableist society. Ableism exists; the world is not built on a scale for me. So, how can we maximize function and independence, and autonomy, and agency—*that* should be the focus rather than looking at fixing my bones and straightening my legs? To be clear, some of that was beneficial, since some interventions allowed me to physically thrive in certain ways. But so much energy—and time and money—was wasted in trying to make me fit and blend into an ableist world. And I just feel that, for me and so many people I know, it's really about function and how I can live on my own terms. How can I make decisions about my care and well-being? What does it mean *to me* to thrive? Not to my doctor or social worker or the other people who will look at it through an ableist lens. What does it mean *to me* to flourish? Let's get there together and have a care partnership that allows that to happen. That is what we need, and I think that's the direction a lot of the medical field engaging with disabled people should go.

Kim Q. Hall:

To add from my experience, when thinking about flourishing on one's own terms and what that means, it's so important *not* to assume heterosexuality or gender. So much of the notion of what it means to "walk" is also about a style of walking; what it means to have a "normal" walk is not about putting one foot in front of the other, but also doing so in a certain way in terms of one's body comportment. The two are fused in my experience of having my walk commented on. I think flourishing involves not separating disability from gender and sexuality. We should always think of people as whole beings and allow for diverse modes of flourishing.

I was an infant, so this is a story told to me, but my parents were upset that I might not ever walk. I think there's a lot that can be done to make it so that people who are making decisions have access to communities and people who can communicate to them that *it's possible to flourish in all kinds of ways of being in the world.* I think that's important, too.

Rod Michalko:

In my experience with the medical community, and as others have told me about theirs, it seems to me that individual practitioners are committed to something that Rosemarie talked about way back in 1997: a *normate* version of the body, of the mind, of the senses, et cetera.[3] The medical community comes to their interactions with us—generally, typically—with that notion of the normate, and that we would, as Kim and Yomi said, like to be anyone other than who we are.

There is that assumption, as Kim said, of our sexuality and gender notions. Medicine sometimes appears to me as the quintessential protector of the normate. It's as if, somehow, I'm an enemy that invaded that. . . . I remember once in graduate school at the University of British Columbia, I had an ophthalmologist look at my eyes. Something was up. So, the ophthalmologist looked at my eyes really close, that kind of thing, and I remember he pushed away and said, "it's really messy in there." I said, "you should see it from this side." And he said not a word. . . .

There needs to be a bit more humanness, a bit more letting go of the normate, letting go of some of the assumptions of what the human, in some kind of a moral sense, ought to be, should be.

Joel Michael Reynolds:

That's really powerful, and it opens directly onto another question from the audience. Each of your talks was in relationship to technology, technologies of multiple sorts, technological interventions, technological objects you use, et cetera. One thing that especially stuck out to an audience member during Rod's talk was the idea that we don't typically think of guide dogs as a technology. Yet, it's also very natural to see why Smokie fits into this conversation and serves an instrumental function in your life, but also is much, much more than merely a technology. I am wondering if you all could talk a bit more about what the concept of technology means to you and how you think about the relationship between your particular way of being disabled, and particularly way of being in the world, and these objects and practices referred to as "technologies."

Rod Michalko:

Sure, Joel, thanks. And thanks for the question. First thing I'd like to say is that my blindness—and disability in general—emerges or becomes a sort of entity or phenomenon because of *the way we relate to it*. So, if I relate to blindness as a technical issue, requiring technical intervention or solution, then my blindness is a technical thing. And, of course, all of us, whether we are disabled or not, can see things in that way. We can see eating food as a technical matter. We all have to use techniques, but they can overpower who we are and can especially overpower a disability identity. One thing nondisabled people harbor is a notion of, "How!?"—"How can they do the stuff I do?" "How can a blind person read?" "How can a wheelchair person get into that building with those stairs?" You have all these notions of *how* we're going to do this stuff. "How can you do the stuff that normates usually do?" It's a fair question. I think Smokie, for instance, was of course a piece of technology insofar as he and I had an instrumental relationship. I relied on him to get around. But more than that, my life was in his hands, really, in some sense. But what Smokie did, more than that, first of all, as the trainers say, he loved to work. He loved to guide. When he heard the harness, he was jumping. He wanted to go to work. He just wanted that. That gave me that sense of joy I was speaking of. *My blindness gave Smokie a chance to do something he loved to do.* It was evident. My blindness became a little bit of a source of joy, for both him and me. It was this bit of blindness Smokie allowed me to bring into the world. It was never this sense of, "Oh, here's a drag, how to get from here to there, and how am I going to do it? How am I going to stay safe?" And there was no, "How am I going to get there?" I enjoyed the trip.

Kim Q. Hall:

It's a great question and very thought provoking. What Rod said was really amazing. We often think of technology as something that we use or that's applied to bodies in order to make it so that bodies can move through conventional kinds of spaces.

There are all kinds of technologies in my experience as well, but when I think about my one example of surgery, and bracing and so on, there are also effects that aren't anticipated in terms of interactions with technologies. In those spaces that are opened up, I think there's a different possibility of being. It's not necessarily applying technology to a body in some way and using it in some way. It also makes something else that wasn't anticipated possible and that also calls into question the more normalizing mode of thinking about technology. That's what is really powerful in terms of having a critical disability critique of technology and what that means.

Joel Michael Reynolds:

This leads us in some ways back to this concept of *crip gain*. It was at play in each of your talks. We got multiple questions about this idea. Some people seemed skeptical. Some seemed confused. Some loved it. All over the board. I would like to return us to this concept and maybe tease it out in a little more detail what does this idea of crip gain mean? If you add all the talks together, there's something about the concept that gets things right, but maybe other things that don't. Ideally, we could do this in a way that ties back to the whole theme of not just this event, but the series as a whole, which is the relationship between disability, technology, and flourishing, this idea that flourishing turns on living the sort of life that one actually wants to.

Kim Q. Hall:

I have my own questions about the term "crip gain." I'm not necessarily comfortable with it. I wasn't trying to say something like, "Oh, just look at all the positive things." I was trying to think of flourishing and using "crip gain" as another word for flourishing and how it is that defying normalization—for example, existing *between* disability and ability—isn't just a scene of loss, but also a scene of flourishing. And I was thinking of how to talk about that in ways that rework an ableist distinction between ability and disability. It's not necessarily about gaining a new skill or something like that. It's about creating *possibilities* for flourishing. And, so, perhaps it isn't the best phrase. I'd be very open and willing to learn from others about that, too.

Yomi Sachiko Young:

Oh, no. I'm going to use it now. From today, going forward, we will be talking about *crip gain*, just like in disability justice spaces where we talk about abolition, resilience, resistance, freedom, joy, and flourishing, and all of that. I really like the concept. You have given me something today, and I'm just going to keep thinking about it.

For me . . . I mentioned something earlier about the protective quality of my wheelchair. I also think about how I've experienced things in this life that I absolutely would not have experienced had I not been born with a disability or acquired a disability or anything. I would not be in this conversation *but for* my specific crip experience. There are millions of other middle-aged black women with whom I share very similar universal experiences. They're not invited into these conversations because what's interesting about me or perhaps what differentiates me is the way I move through the world; it's this positioning of myself as outside "the normal way" of things. I see that as a gain. I just like this concept of all the ways that my disability has provided access into spaces and experiences that I wouldn't otherwise have. But, also, I see my experience of who I am as Yomi as deeply spiritual. I feel it's an exercise of spirituality that I am on. I'm working out a lot of things in this lifetime, on this plane, at this moment right now. I feel like this is the body and experience I was meant to have. I like this concept of crip gain because when I review all of the things I have been through, all of the things I've experienced and the way my mind and heart have been sharpened and smoothed over and over again by these experiences I have, I see that as *gain*. I see that as something I've been endowed and blessed with.

Rod Michalko:

That's beautiful, Yomi. I have some of Kim's and Yomi's understanding and feel about gain. I think what's interesting to me is that the gain I get from blindness isn't what people usually think. It's not that I gain better hearing or touch. The gain I got was the understanding that being on the margins of life is, as Yomi hinted at and, as bell hooks used to say, not such a bad thing. It's just not too bad of a position to be in. You can see a lot of stuff from the margins that you can't see from the centers, to use that metaphor.

As Yomi says, I would not be here at all if not for my blindness and if not for who I am, in that sense. Blindness is just a part of who I am, and not "what" I am. It's not something that attached itself to me. It's me and part of who I am. It has also given me a sense of looking at the center in a way that being smack dab in the middle of it doesn't really give you. It's like that old-fashioned saying that a fish has no idea it's in water ... it gave me a chance to ask a question and revisit a question my partner and disability studies colleague, Tanya Titchkosky, once asked: "Once we, as disabled people, are in, what are we in for?"

That kind of question centers this visceral need to include us. Now "inclusion" has gone from an act to a thing these days. It's amazing how badly they want us in. I am thinking about another blind scholar, Devon Healey, in regard to inclusion: to get in is one thing; to stay in is another. It's almost as if we were saying that once we're included, if we want to stick around, we need to bring our own glue.

Yomi Sachiko Young:

Thinking more about gains, there's some fan fiction that people with my disability have these super brains ... that people with osteogenesis imperfecta (OI) are super intelligent and articulate, great communicators. And, of course, I was told this growing up in terms of, "hey, this is a positive!" That's fine, and I believed it was true because I was reading at a very young age. I started memorizing books at two years old. I could recite them back. I was very conversant. I was a good and clear communicator. I met a lot of other children with OI who were the same way. It just seemed that we had these super brains, and that it was something we gained as having a congenital disability. Later on, my orthopedic specialist at Stanford, Dr. James Gamble and I were talking about this. He would ask what I do, where I go to school, and what my job was. He would want to know people's position and trajectory and whether they "carried the smart gene." He told me something fascinating and that I believe is true. It is not that we have super brains. But because our bodies are fragile (I was *born* with several broken bones, and it's not unusual for people with my disability to break hundreds of bones in our lifetime). Because of always being in peril physically, we had to develop language early in order to communicate danger, pain, fear, how to handle us, how and where to move us; *it's an adaptation*. I believe it probably caries through to a lot of other disabilities to develop early verbal skills. It's not because of big brains, but due to the adaptation, the need to be able to communicate to anyone touching or handling us the right way to do it so that we were not repeatedly injured. I see that as a gain.

Joel Michael Reynolds:

Thank you, Yomi. A number of people asked about the relationship between gender and disability. There were also a number of questions concerning race and ethnicity, and it seems that a number of audience members are eager to hear thoughts on how to think about these things together or perhaps how to think about them separately whilst keeping the focus on disability . . . how we might envision a truly intersectional understanding of what disability looks like.

Kim Q. Hall:

In terms of gender and disability—let's start there, but thinking more broadly about class, race, and disability as well—when we think about what body norms are, they're always already gendered. There's a way to move. There's a way to be embodied and to gesture—those are always gendered modes. Disability places one outside of those gendered norms as well, as does being gender nonconforming and queer—all of which places one outside of expectations about the body, heterosexuality, and gender conformity. The performance of heterosexuality and gender conformity in one's navigation of the world is also *a performance of ability*. I think that's what Robert McRuer talks about regarding compulsory able-bodiedness and compulsory heterosexuality and how they rely on each other. Their normalization and naturalization depend on each other. Walking is one site where they come together in terms of how I move and navigate the world, and how my modes and navigation are responded to, whether that's by a stare or comment. One is always aware that you're not quite what people expect you to be.

Also, thinking about race and class . . . how there are ways in which, in a white supremacist context, as a white person, I have more fluid movement in the world. We're always in those conditioned spaces, between moving through the world in an unobstructed way and being perceived as not belonging in it. That environment needs to be navigated as well. It's part of what is navigated.

Joel Michael Reynolds:

That's wonderful, Kim. It brings me back to this theme that I heard in each of the talks of the *betweenness*, the aspect of not necessarily being on one side or the "other" of a phenomenon, norm, expectation, or even how one relates to oneself. And that one of the aspects of many sorts of disability experiences involves feeling in the margins.

Yomi Sachiko Young:

The way I think about all this and apply certain practices is by being a student of and learning more about how to embody a disability justice framework, which is intersectional and centers the most impacted and picks up where the disability rights movement left off... where we're explicitly naming racism, sexism, and gender violence, all of these things, as identities and experiences that we shouldn't have to rank or check at the door in order to have rights or to be free. There are ten principles to disability justice in that framework that I think really illuminate what you and Kim were just talking about.[4] It's where my political heart and home are these days: in really understanding my place in the world and where I see the work being. The work is toward liberation. The work is anticapitalist and abolitionist, to tear down white supremacy and ableism. That work is led by people of color, queer people, folks who are neurodiverse, people who haven't been the standard bearers of the disability rights movement.

Joel Michael Reynolds:

That is a perfect way to end this conversation. I want to add one thing to what you said so wonderfully, Yomi. When we talked about ableism earlier, I should have said that the best understanding of that term, in my opinion, is from Talila Lewis.[5] Lewis also worked with Dustin Gibson and a collective of people to come up with a version of ableism that takes settler colonialism seriously, anti-Black racism seriously, capitalism seriously, and so much more. It's really a genius understanding of the term.

Yomi Sachiko Young:

Those are our luminary thinkers: Stacey Milburn, Patti Berne, Leroy Moore, Mia Mingus. These are the people who gave us this gift of the disability justice framework. And we have so many others, as you've named, who are carrying that work forward. They are the guiding lights for us and for me.

Joel Michael Reynolds:

Yes. And all of you are guiding lights as well.

3

Disrupting Ableism with Artful Activism

Lateef McLeod and D.J. Savarese

Liz Bowen:

Welcome to "Disrupting Ableism with Artful Activism," the third event in our series *The Art of Flourishing: Conversations on Disability*, which is generously supported by the National Endowment for the Humanities. My name is Liz Bowen, and I'm the Rice Family Postdoctoral Fellow in Bioethics and the Humanities at The Hastings Center and one of the co-organizers of this series.

We are so excited to have you here with us today and look forward to our conversation. Without further ado, I will turn things over to my colleague Erik Parens, senior research scholar at The Hastings Center and director of the series.

Erik Parens:

Thank you, Liz, for your invaluable substantive and technical contributions to creating this event. And thanks to all of you for joining this third event in our series, *The Art of Flourishing*. The purpose of this Hastings Center series is to broadcast and explore one fundamental theme, which is that people can flourish in all sorts of bodyminds. (Different from our first two events, where we referred to simply to "bodies," we are now following critical disability scholars such as Margaret Price and referring to "bodyminds"[1] to indicate our awareness that what we usually call our "bodies" and what we usually call our "minds" are two aspects of the unique unity that is each of us.) To "flourish" means to exercise the capacities we have in pursuit of the goals that we find meaningful. None of us needs a different bodymind to flourish.

Because the term "bioethics" can have negative connotations for some people with disabilities, I want to say a bit more about what doing bioethics has meant at The Hastings Center. Since its inception, many of us at Hastings have been thinking critically about the meaning of very familiar medical technologies like those monitors with the red digital numbers that often hover above our heads when we're patients in hospital beds. The concern has been that in drawing doctors' attention to a single feature of how someone's body is functioning, such technologies can take doctors' attention away from the whole person. And bioethicists at Hastings have been concerned that emerging reproductive technologies like prenatal genetic testing are being used to ensure that only people with certain sorts of bodyminds will be welcomed into the human community. And we have been concerned that medical professionals sometimes foist onto people with atypical bodies very old-fashioned technologies like leg braces, with a view to fixing people who in fact need no fixing at all. So, we at Hastings have often emphasized that such technologies have been integral parts of systems that can thwart the flourishing of many people, in particular disabled people. And I want to acknowledge that in developing such critiques, we have not always given equal attention to the myriad ways that people in general and disabled people in particular use both old-fashioned and brand-new technologies to promote their own flourishing.

Fortunately, our two featured presenters today, poets and activists Lateef McLeod and D.J. Savarese, push us at

Hastings—even more than the speakers at our first two events pushed us—to remember the ways in which augmentative and alternative communication (AAC) technologies enable our presenters to promote their own flourishing. Augmentative and alternative communication technologies, for those of you who don't already know, are technologies that enable people to communicate in language without the use of vocal cords or hand signing. Moreover, Lateef and D.J. push us to notice that despite Hastings' long-standing commitment to critiquing our culture's excessive devotion to the value of *in*dependence, the language we have used to describe our series could be interpreted to suggest that we ourselves remain excessively devoted to that value. That is to say, claiming that people can promote their own flourishing could be interpreted to be a sign that, despite our own best intentions, we at Hastings too remain in thrall to the fantasy of independence. More specifically, Lateef and D.J. will challenge us to imagine a world in which we all remember that everyone's ability to exercise their capacities in the ways that they want depends decisively on our *inter*dependence.

Lateef and D.J. will challenge us to remember that our ability to exercise our capacities depends decisively on the fact that we are all embedded in webs of relationships with others. You might say that they will challenge us to imagine a world in which we all get to pursue our own flourishing, but in full awareness of the sense in which *our flourishing is never simply our own*.

Not only will these two poets and activists present how they imagine our shared future, but they will give us examples of how they and others are using various art forms to disrupt the stereotypes, stigmatization, and discrimination—that is, the ableism—that stands between the world we all inhabit now and the one they invite us all to imagine. It's now my great pleasure to turn the mic over to Ralph Savarese, who is a professor of English at Grinnell College, as well as an essayist, poet, and activist.

Ralph Savarese:

Thank you, Erik, for the introduction. So, it's really my great pleasure to introduce Lateef McLeod, a poet, novelist, scholar, performer, and activist. He earned a BA in English from the University of California, Berkeley, and an MFA in Creative Writing from Mills College. He is currently in the doctoral program in anthropology and social change at the California Institute of Integral Studies in San Francisco. He has published two books of poetry, *A Declaration of a Body of Love* in 2010 and *Whispers of Krip Love, Shouts of Krip Revolution* in 2020. He is currently at work on a novel titled *The Third Eye Is Crying*. He has had a long affiliation with the disability justice performance project Sins Invalid, which centers people of color, queer people, nonbinary people, and trans people with disabilities. He performed in the 2007, 2011, 2016, and 2020 shows. In 2011, he was the project's artist in residence, and, in 2020, he appeared in *We Love Like Barnacles: Crip Lives in Climate Chaos*. This show focused on the intersection between climate justice and disability justice, and the word "crip" in the performance title, Lateef says, was used as an inclusive, reclaimed term for disabled people. Lateef's piece in the show, entitled "Running from the Ecological Wave," explored the theme of communication that has been so central to his work as a self-advocate, writer, and poet. Last year, he started a podcast titled *Black Disabled Men Talk* with cohosts Leroy Moore, one of our questioners today; Keith Jones; and Otis Smith. You can find this podcast at http://www.blackdisabledmentalk.com/.

Lateef's community service work and activism includes serving as the cochair of the Persons with Disabilities Ministry at Allen Temple Baptist Church, and as the vice president of the Leadership Committee and Executive Board member of the International Society for Augmentative and Alternative Communication. He recently joined the Board of the Alliance for Citizen-Directed Supports. "I bring the same passion," Lateef says, "and zeal to the

Board of the Alliance, along with my insights from self-advocacy and perspective as a person who uses AAC and is a Black man with cerebral palsy. I wish to highlight the experiences of people of color with disabilities in this country."

In a poem titled "Wall," Lateef says wittily, though with an edge, "I can't use my 3000 dollar lightwriter as a paperweight." And then the poem turns darker, referencing what disability theorists have called "crip time," which presents such a challenge to the able-bodied who value speed and productivity. "A tortoise tries to crawl a race with a bullet train / [. . .] can't we just find a fiber optic way / to hook my brain to the machine / so my thoughts can be electronically voiced [. . .]" In this poem, speed and stigma become a war that Lateef tries desperately to break down. "I shiver behind this clear wall," he writes, "and wait for someone to notice me / wait for a chance to speak." How fortunate we jabberers are to slow down today and hear the words of such a profound and masterful poet. Please join me in welcoming Lateef McLeod. Thank you.

Lateef McLeod:

Thank you for that introduction, Ralph. I am Lateef McLeod. And for a visible description of myself, I am a Black man with cerebral palsy and low-cut hair, a mustache, and a beard. I am wearing a dark, blue-and-brown checkered blazer and a light blue shirt with black stripes. I am sitting in a Permobil power wheelchair in front of a bookcase. Now I will begin my talk.

It is obvious to say that people with disabilities occupy a marginal and subordinate position in the United States. Our society has largely developed in the last two hundred years without taking much consideration of how people with disabilities would fit in and live in the communities that were developing in the United States in the nineteenth century. Some U.S. cities passed laws and ordinances that were known as "ugly laws," which barred people with disabilities from being seen on public streets.[2] This legal discrimination of people with disabilities in public venues and other public spaces proceeded until the United States passed a series of disability rights laws starting approximately forty years ago. However, even with the passing of disability rights law such as the Americans with Disabilities Act (ADA) and innovation with assistive technology that assists people with disabilities with their daily lives, the disability community still faces marginalization in today's society, whether it is in the job market or other areas.

While many people think that assistive technology and policy changes are the solutions to these inequities, these efforts are not adequate to address the profound cultural stigma that attends disability. Therefore, people with disabilities need to look beyond these approaches to achieve equity and continue to strive for substantially revolutionary change. The disability community is full of potential but faces many barriers in becoming integrated into today's society. People with disabilities experience lower rates of employment than people without disabilities. For example, in 2019, the employment population ratio for people with disabilities was 19.3%, compared to the ratio for those without disabilities, which was 66.3%.[3]

With people with disabilities largely out of work, the population has a significant barrier in integrating into the dominant culture, where having a job is the prime indicator of if someone is a contributing member of her or his society. People in the disability community are still building their presence in the societal public sphere so that they can finally have a sense of belonging instead of being ignored. Historically, mainstream society has not been designed with people with disabilities in mind, and it has barely adjusted to accommodate us. In addition to banning us from the streets, this country has a long history of keeping people with disabilities in medical institutions. This is primarily due to our society's view of disability based on the medical model, which treats one's impairments as an individual problem that should be fixed with using medical solutions that adapt the person as closely as possible to societal body norms. In contrast, and as a reaction to the medical model, the disability community has been promoting the social model of disability, in which the disabled body is not deemed deficient but, instead, the social environment of a community must be adapted to become more accessible to disabled people.

There is also the disability justice model, which adds on to the social model of disability by arguing that disability is just one facet of a disabled person's identity, among other facets like race and gender that she or he has to negotiate in this identity-driven, hierarchical society. Disability justice states that for true disability liberation to occur, we, of course, need to dismantle the capitalist system that totally devalues disabled bodies and minds. An outgrowth of this devaluing is transhumanism, a philosophy promoting the idea of eventually erasing disability with human augmented technology. They believe that with science and technology, they can perfect the human mind and body and blot out any imperfections to the human anatomy. This erasure of disability ignores all the positive contributions disabled people and disabled culture bring to our society.

As a society, we should not strive to erase disability, but to build our society such that disability is one of the central considerations when establishing a community. This will only happen with greater respect for disability, having the heightened value of people with disability's point of view. Essentially, we also need a disabled-led movement so that society is accessible for everyone. When this happens, people will not be defined by the labor that they can or cannot do, but by the relationships that they cultivate and the contributions they make in their community. This is how a disability liberation can come to fruition, and it will necessitate a huge cultural shift in society.

The main impediment to this cultural shift is that disabled people are perceived as other in our society. Disability policy and other positive developments for the disability community mitigate but do not erase the ableism that disabled people face on a daily basis. To imagine what it would take to disrupt ableism, it helps to recognize four ways in which disabled people are still seen today. There is the victim stereotype, the innocent stereotype, the villain stereotype, and the super crip stereotype.

The victim stereotype portrays disabled people as helpless and vulnerable because of their disability. The public reacts to this stereotype by treating a person with a disability like an object of pity that should be ignored. A popular version of this stereotype is seen in the Shriners Hospitals for Children commercials seen on CNN, which depict people with disabilities as needing charity to prosper and engage in daily activities.

The innocent stereotype in the literature and other media is the character with an intellectual disability who is portrayed as childlike and dependent on others. This stereotype explains why people with intellectual disabilities are treated like children; they are deemed not to have the cognitive ability to be a functioning adult. This stereotype affects many people with disabilities like cerebral palsy or autism, whether they have a cognitive disability or not. A good example of this is the *Forrest Gump* movie, whose main character had an intellectual disability.

At the same time that some disabled people are portrayed as overly innocent, however, the villain stereotype portrays them as dangerous and evil because of their disability. This stereotype is found in films which depict people with psychological disabilities as dangerous and murderous. The stereotype explains why people with these types of disabilities are stigmatized in society and are sometimes subjected to police murder at higher rates than nondisabled people. An example of this is the character Elijah Grace, also known as Mr. Glass, who had brittle bones and played the villain in the movie *Unbreakable* and had intentions of doing battle with the hero of the film, David Dunn.

Lastly, the super crip stereotype is portrayed as a disabled person overcoming his or her disability, introducing amazing feats. A good example of someone who epitomized this trope before his legal trouble was Oscar Pistorius, who was a Paralympic professional sprinter who competed in the regular Olympics. This stereotype is used to silence other disabled people, and it does this by pointing to these disabled people that accomplish exceptional feats as proof that the playing field is level and fair for everyone. It is also meant to signify to disabled people that they can achieve a level of able-bodied normalization if they put effort into it.

As I've said earlier in my lecture, these types of sentiments are not true. If ableism is to be dismantled in this culture, these stereotypes must be sufficiently demolished. Since ableism and stereotypes about disability are so prevalent in our dominant culture, people with disabilities must be able to organize and struggle to change these cultural norms. There is another narrative that must be constructed that illustrates the full, multifaceted humanity of people with disabilities to a wider public. Disabled writers, artists, and activists have the great challenge of illustrating to the rest of society what it means to be disabled in America. As cultural workers, we need to construct and articulate what a society would look like if disabled people are not the subordinate category in our culture, and what it would mean that people with disabilities had a strengthened sense of self determination in our society.

Organizations like Sins Invalid and Krip-Hop Nation take up this mantle already, offering disabled artists a platform to exhibit their work in art, music, and theater. Sins Invalid specifically looks at the intersectionality of disability, sexuality, and performance art. They make the principles of disability justice alive through their theater work, and they offer a vision of what disability liberation will look like in re-enactments on stage. They revolutionarily perform positive examples of disability sexuality onstage.

The sexuality of disabled people has long been a source of taboo in this society with our history of eugenics, but Sins Invalid illustrates on stage that disabled bodies and sexualities are beautiful and should be celebrated. Krip-Hop Nation, led by Leroy Moore, centers writers, musicians, and artists of color with disabilities for

Black and brown communities, and highlights and showcases their work, making it visible to a wider public. Leroy Moore saw that disabled musicians were not getting much exposure in the mainstream industry and thought to produce an alternative platform where more people could be exposed to these disabled musicians' and artists' work. Disabled cultural workers have to offer stories and real-life examples of disabled people living full lives in our society while offering strategies to help. These types of stories of disabled people living their lives can be expanded to include more stories of disabled people with intersectional identities giving their life perspectives. They can also lead their communities in conceptualizing possible futures where disabled people can have a complete liberated potentiality. These ideas may be considered radical at this moment in time, but they can be normalized with disabled artists, writers, and intellectuals constantly promoting them. Once the mainstream public sees more positive and realistic images of disabled people, their conceptions about disabled people will change, and this will hopefully lessen the level of ableism disabled people experience in society.

We can collectively imagine what a liberated society for disabled people will look like. What will this mean, and how can we accomplish having most of the adult population that wants to work incorporated into the job market? How will it look if we have prominent disabled leaders in society that we all look up to and respect? How will it change society if more people see and engage with disabled people in their community? What old misconceptions and outdated cultural norms do we as a society have to discard as disabled people gain more social power in society? These are questions we have to answer as this century progresses. These are questions that our activists like Patty Berne, Leroy Moore, Keah Brown, Alice Wong, and Keith Jones are starting to answer for us with their artistic, literary, and political work. These disabled cultural workers and many others will take the lead in framing what this potential future will look like. Our goal will be to help future generations who will be born with disabilities to not be oppressed by that identity, but to have every opportunity and right to lead fulfilled lives, like everyone should.

Rosemarie Garland-Thomson:

Thank you, everyone, for being here today with us. I have the honor of introducing my friend and colleague David James Savarese. D.J. is a poet and artful activist, a public scholar, and a self-described practicing optimist.

D.J. Savarese has had a distinctive and distinguished educational and creative career that I want to detail for you here as my introduction. D.J. started becoming the writer that he is today early on. At the age of six, he began what he calls "actively disrupting the status quo" when he exited the foster care system and a segregated center for kids with disabilities to attend a regular kindergarten class in his new neighborhood school. D.J. is now one of two alternatively communicating American Autistics who were fully included throughout their educational career from kindergarten through college. During his first year of high school, he continued these status quo disruptions by giving us one of the best disability justice lines, in my view, in all social media.

In an interview on the *Anderson Cooper 360°* show, which was about autism and possible medical cures, the doctor-journalist Sanjay Gupta asked D.J., "Should autism be treated?" and without skipping a beat, fifteen-year-old D.J. replied, "Yes. Treated with respect."

D.J. went on to graduate Phi Beta Kappa in 2017 from Oberlin College, where he lived on campus in the dorm and frequently hosted creative arts salons. He double majored in anthropology and creative writing and concentrated in geology and somatic studies. Both his honors thesis and his capstone poetry project won awards. When I asked D.J. why he studied these subjects, he told me, and

I quote, "I loved the way modern-day anthropology asks the writer to reflect on what they didn't know that they didn't know to call out their own ethnocentric assumptions. Creative writing," D.J. went on to tell me, "offered me the opportunity to continue writing in my native language; and geology," he continued, "gave me a way to read the Earth's stories and understand its signatures."

D.J. is now a widely published and recognized artful activist. He's written a book called *A Doorknob for the Eye*. He has a notable Best American essay and an insightful piece called "Coming to My Senses." He is most well-known for being the coproducer, narrative commentator, and subject of the Peabody Award–winning documentary called *Deej: Inclusion Shouldn't Be a Lottery*. He also founded Listen to Us: Writing Our Own Futures when he was an Open Society Foundation Human Rights Initiative Youth Fellow.

Currently, D.J. is collaborating with artist Malcolm Corley and fellow poets Claretta Holsey, Lateef McLeod, and Jorrell Watkins on a forthcoming book on poetry and art. D.J. also teaches and presents nationally on a range of topics. His autoethnographic study entitled "Unearthing the Tools and the Concepts" is forthcoming as a collaboration, as is a collaboration with his father, Ralph, on life-writing across genres. As a working board member of the Alliance for Citizen Directed Supports, he is spearheading a national collection of narratives and pathways entitled Lives-in-Progress. I'm pleased now to present my colleague and friend D.J. Savarese.

D.J. Savarese:

Thank you, Rosemarie. Hi, everyone. My name is David James Savarese. I am a white man in my twenties with glasses; a goatee; and short, reddish-brown hair, wearing a quarter-zip gray and blue sweater. As a former foster child, I know what it's like to fight hard not to be thrown away and forgotten. As an optimist, I believe not only that nobody is disposable, but that everybody is indispensable. We are all essential and meaningful participants of something larger than ourselves. Lateef, in your talk, you made the case for a cultural revolution led by the disabled for the disabled and asked each of us to envision a world in which every body and every voice is indispensable.

Today, I'd like to explore how creative forms of resistance, what I call "artful activism," can be used to disrupt cultural misperceptions of the disabled, unearth deep-seated assumptions that bury us, and seed possibilities for lasting cultural change: in short, how artful activism allows us not just to exist in the world we're given but to create new ways of being for and with ourselves *and others*. And I'll use my documentary film, *Deej: Inclusion Shouldn't Be a Lottery*, to illustrate.

First, allow me to more intimately acquaint you with who I am. I identify as an alternatively communicating synesthete, a severely apraxic autistic with, as Jill Magi would say, "nerve endings 'out to there' beyond [my] physical bod[y] . . . and [I] write from that experience, that stance of beyond-borders, beyond momentary agency."[4] What does that mean?

It means I belong to a vast ecosystem, not simply to some city or state or country, not just to some gender, ethnicity, race, or class, but to the universe, a vast place ultimately devoid of any man-made borders. It means to me the world is astonishingly—sometimes even confusingly—alive. The categories "human" and "nonhuman" crumble like a sandcastle at the beach, and the white, frothy wave of my attention spreads generously over everything. And because I need help to do things neurotypicals take for granted, from tying my shoes to wiping my mouth, my sense of agency is much less individualistic, much less human-centered. I see that we are all interdependent, not independent, that we yearn for self-efficacy, not self-reliance. That means we need to pay attention to the *how* of what we do. It's not enough to simply climb up the dominant culture's power structure to be included.

I often refer to ableism as the cultivated garden of a speech-based society. If I adopt that model as a given—as the only way of being—then my only hope to avoid being weeded out, so to speak, is to become an exception to the rule. But if, instead, I see life as a field of diverse and interconnected rhizomes—what some might call weeds—then I begin to undermine what keeps us dutifully stuck in an inclusion–exclusion coupling, in which some beings are seen as disposable and others not.

What is it about rhizomes? Well, unlike so-called true roots, which have single roots and stems, rhizomes persevere by creating an intricate network of multiple root bulbs full of nutrients and resources that grow both vertically and laterally. If cut down, they grow back. Faced with adverse conditions, they can lie dormant underground for up to a year, rejuvenating themselves before blossoming again. In this sense, weeding them out is far more difficult, if not impossible. With no center or defined boundaries, a rhizome grows in multiple directions simultaneously, disregarding the artificial borders in its path. Rhizomes are as diverse as bamboo, turmeric, and iris.

We can't change who we are, but we can change the hopeful ways we relate to each other. Law, policy, and many assistive technologies assume the disabled are outsiders striving to inhabit that cultivated garden. They seek to offer us passage across the divide by dismantling the physical barriers and by helping us pass or pose as independent, able-bodied speakers. But once there, we are seen as exceptional and accepting of the status quo. But what if, like rhizomes, we see ourselves as one of many lives-in-progress and seek to identify and disrupt the attitudinal barriers that keep members of the dominant culture imprisoned behind that garden wall? What if, instead of making our way into the garden, we invite everyone out into the field? What might that look like?

With these questions in mind, let's talk about how film and poetry and oil paint animation came together in the making of my documentary film, *Deej: Inclusion Shouldn't Be a Lottery*. Although we won our funding and a Peabody Award for our unprecedented commitment to inclusive filmmaking, we began the editorial process firmly entrenched in the cultivated garden of mainstream cinema, where the filmmaker reimagines himself as a neutral reporter and invites me to respond to his questions under the auspices of his knowing better what the audience would want or need to know. So, the first thing we needed to do was disrupt the editing process and position me as the questioner, trusting the audience to be ready, willing, and able to confront the limitations of their perspectives, even if the filmmaker wasn't yet there himself. This freed me to use the narrative voice to talk back, to challenge the camera's gaze, to prove it was in fact not a neutral force, and to begin answering the questions the filmmaker would never have imagined asking. To our credit, by the time the film reached its final form, we actually opted to make this tension between filmmaker and subject an overt part of the film.

However, the biggest obstacle still remained: the narrative structure itself. The filmmaker had a traditional sense of a "will-he-make-it" narrative that felt essentializing to me, and he argued that the formation of events into episodes is mere storytelling and fell strictly within his purview as filmmaker. I, as the subject of the film, argued that the plot is an integral part of self-representation and identity formation, and strove for the fluidity and multivocality of a narrative identity that configures and reconfigures itself, full of contradictions and growth, as various layers intersect and influence each other.

I realized that no amount of narrative commentary could subvert the overarching "will-he-make-it" narrative. I needed something to disrupt its steadfast linearity, and I found my answer in my native language. Poetry, with its foregrounding of the sensorial and the metaphorical, offers the closest alphabetical translation to my experience. It moves associatively, not linearly. It finds commonalities about seemingly disparate things. It doesn't just make broad claims and ask details to be subordinate. Poetry communicates with the reader in a way that alters both of us. It seeds possibility, encourages people to open up. Because it's multimodal and activates the senses, poetry dislodges us from a strictly meaning-based experience and frees ideas to mingle across boundaries of the brain. In this way, people can let go of and move beyond preconceived abstract concepts; artificial, classificatory constructions of power; and mere exercises in political correctness. In short, poetry opens us up to be less didactic. And if poetry is what lured me into language in the first place, perhaps it could be used to lure the audience into the field.

So, the first thing we did was plant four of my poems throughout the film. The question then became how to find a cinematic companion to the poems without simply illustrating or overpowering them. A lengthy search led to Em Cooper, a British director, an artist specializing in oil paint animation. As we worked together, I realized that the animation could function as a foil to the realistic mode of the film, inviting viewers to get beyond what the camera appears to register about autism. Because the camera can't help but stare, another visual medium might better align with the autist's point of view.

Em Cooper says it this way: "On reading D.J.'s poem 'Swoon,' my mind was flooded by his descriptions of the visceral union of his sensory experience. His words had such breathtaking clarity, they sprang to life in my mind, and I felt as though I could see the poem. The challenge D.J. and I began to tackle together was how to create a sense of that reading mind's eye on screen. I wanted to create an atmosphere to underlie the poem, to hold the space so that D.J.'s words could have their powerful effect on the viewer. Another aim was to find a way of using the animation to create openings within the objective onlooking of the live action film to hint at a more subjective point of view. I have found that the slippery combination of oil paint and live action gives an opportunity for this: images can form and melt, sliding into one another like fleeting thoughts. Punctuating the film with these sequences reminds us that the footage we see through the camera lens is only the exterior."

But Em Cooper didn't stop with simply reading the poems. We met by Google Chat every week. She read every paper and poem I'd written in my time at Oberlin. Rather than illustrate the poem, images from my writing—of volcanoes, flags, and vines—surface, then disappear, only to resurface in the next poem. The viewers are literally swept into the vortex and back out again, ever closer to the garden's perimeter. Without her wordless encouragement or sensory accommodation, the viewer's transformations would not have been complete. When it came time to choose my voice to read the poems, I found myself up against that garden wall again. All the filmmakers wanted a dramatic reading by some actor I had never met. I wanted a voice I knew and trusted, one that had lured me back into the field. So, I chose the person responsible for me bringing nature so fully into my writing and being: that of my ecopoetics professor, writing mentor, and closest confidante. We worked and worked together until it sounded just like the words as I heard them when I placed them in the poem. Let's pause for a second now and watch "Swoon" together as it opens the film.

* * *

AUDIO DESCRIPTION: . . .Types on a laptop, one keystroke at a time with his right index finger. In animation, the keyboard morphs into a liquid stream of vegetation and other constantly changing images.

POET: The ear that hears the cardinal / hears in red; // the eye that spots the salmon / sees in wet. // My senses always fall in love: / they spin, swoon; they lose themselves in one / another's arms. // Your senses live alone / like bachelors, // like bitter, slanted rhymes, whose / marriage is a sham.

AUDIO DESCRIPTION: Stairs become tall buildings.

POET: They greet the world the way accountants / greet their books.
AUDIO DESCRIPTION: A red flag becomes a swirling blanket. A hand pushes it away.
POET: I tire of such mastery. And yet, my senses / often fail // to let me do the simplest things, / like walk outside.
AUDIO DESCRIPTION: The door opens onto a sunny lawn.
POET: Invariably, the sun invades / my ears // and terrifies my feet—the angular assault of Heaven's // heavy metal chords. / I cannot hear // to see, cannot see to move. / And so I cling, // As on a listing ship at night, / to the stair-rail.
AUDIO DESCRIPTION: The animation comes to rest on a green vine wrapped around a branch. It dissolves away, and the young, bespectacled man with reddish brown hair and a thin beard stares at the words on the screen.

* * *

D.J. Savarese:

I leave viewers at the end of my documentary film with the reminder that hope lives on, messy and imperfect. I say this because hope takes work. We need to nurture it by meaningfully engaging with others about what matters. Each success fosters our belief in ourselves. If we're hopeful, we're open to other ideas. We're making a difference in others' lives, not just our own. We've all read about ecosystems unwittingly devastated by us humans removing some element, some being, from its natural environment to "benefit" the well-being of some other inhabitants. The pandemic has shed light on our common practice of doing this, even to one another. The American and ableist ideals of self-reliance and independence position us as adversaries vying for ownership over a scarcity of resources. What if, instead, we experienced ourselves as part of the intricate web of interdependence that is our ecosystem, acknowledging that we make the world a better place when each one of us has the freedom to breathe and to grow?

Ralph Savarese:

Thank you, D.J. I will be managing the questions in the first half of the program. We will have a mix of pre-asked questions with prerecorded answers and spontaneous questions from the audience and spontaneous answers, and they'll be interwoven so that there's less time just spent typing and in order to give D.J. and Lateef sufficient time to answer.

So, I'll ask the first question for Lateef. The Canadian poet Jordan Scott has sought "to explore stuttering poetically." His book *Blurt* purposefully sabotages fluency by making it hard for him to read aloud. Stuttering becomes less a disability than a force that beautifully bends language. For him, "[e]very word is achieved through bodily negotiation." Could you talk, Lateef, about the relationship between your own poetry and embodiment? What difference does disability make in the making of words?

Lateef McLeod:

I make a conscious effort to capture my body of experience on the page in my poetry and my other writings. The poetic verse allows me to explain to the reader or the listener the dynamics of my disability and how it is being in my body. A perfect example of this is my poem "Absence of Routine," where I explain what it is like to always be conscious of how I need to swallow my saliva. I structured my poem so at the end of the poem, I repeatedly interrupt the flow of the poem with the word "swallow" to illustrate how I always need to think of swallowing when I am in my body. So, I try to offer the reader a real tactile response to what having a disability is like.

Ralph Savarese:

Thank you, Lateef. So now I'll ask the first question from the audience for D.J. "There is a saying that we can judge a society based on how the society treats its lesser or weaker members. However, people with disabilities are actually among the strongest and greatest members of a society. Please comment on how your life experience, including dealing with challenges, has made you strong."

D.J. Savarese:

I'm strongest when I'm rhizomatically connected with many people and projects. My strength was something I brought with me from foster care. I've been meaningfully engaged in many projects and have gained a sense of self-efficacy, the belief that I can create a meaningful difference.

Janice Lowe:

Thank you for this conversation. D.J., you write of your personal experience with interdependence and of interdependence as an aspirational value for society. How has your filmmaking collaboration informed your ideas about societal interdependence as an antidote for ableism?

D.J. Savarese:

I love this question, Janice. Thank you for asking it. Thank you for using the word "antidote." Ableism is indeed poisoning many beings within our ecosystem. I want to begin by clarifying that interdependence isn't a theory or aspiration for me, but rather the underlying truth of any ecosystem. I also want to clarify that I think independence is a myth, and a dangerous one, at this point in our lives and in the life of our planet, whereas interdependence is a mutually beneficial, fluid way of being.

Now, to get back to your question. It's less about me discovering interdependence during the film collaboration and more about me insisting on it. As we began editing more than seventy hours of film into fifty-four- and seventy-two-minute versions, we found ourselves at odds quite a bit. The filmmakers' choices were creating a story about my parents or my grandparents as my only source of strength. But it's less that than my wanting to be connected with many different sources of strength and, in turn, to be a source of strength for them. I'm not where I am solely because of my parents, and saying that I am actually cuts off possibilities for anyone less fortunate than myself. I am where I am because I soundly insisted on relating with many, many, many, many different people, and because I worked hard to help many other people best their misassumptions. So, we teach people it's all about them, but it's not. It's all about becoming essential to the larger world. That's why I insisted on having as many different people and relationships included in the film as possible, and it's why I'm offering the various communities in which I live more than just someone who needs them.

As I mentioned in my talk, I did find interdependence in my collaboration with Em Cooper and Marco Wilkinson in the making of the poems and oil paint animation. And I'm grateful my poems and oil paint animation embody that essential interdependence.

Ralph Savarese:

Thank you, D.J. And now a question from the audience for Lateef. What advice would you give to a disabled person who is a poet and disability awareness activist who hopes to publish their work and perform more? How do you deal with things like writer's block and rejection?

Lateef McLeod:

I would advise them to get a literary agent because they will direct them to publishing opportunities. [...] I wish I had that when publishing my books.

Rayna Rapp:

Hi, Lateef, and thank you for your comprehensive overview of the many facets of ableism in U.S. life. You've given us some wonderful examples of how disability artful activism breaks through stereotypes and other ableist barriers in the works of Sins Invalid and Krip-Hop Nation. Can you tell us a little bit about how a disability artful activist perspective informs your own work? Can you ... read us one of your poems? That would be wonderful.

Lateef McLeod:

The disability art activist perspective informs my work because I consider myself an artist and a writer before being a scholar. As a result, much of my thinking is influenced by my engagement in creative work. The creative work of Sins Invalid and Krip-Hop Nation heavily influences my work. I'm participating in both Sins Invalid and Krip-Hop Nation projects, which have made me grow as an intellectual and an artist. I firmly believe that our artistry expands our intellectual thinking, and I intentionally use my art to expand the possibility for disability liberation. Now I will read my poem, "I Am Too Pretty for Some Ugly Laws":

I Am Too Pretty for Some Ugly Laws.

I am not supposed to be here / in this body, / here / speaking to you. / My mere presence / of erratic moving limbs / and drooling smile / used to be scrubbed / off the public pavement. // Ugly Laws used to be / in many U.S. cities' law books / beginning in Chicago in 1867, / stating that "any person who is / diseased, maimed, mutilated, / or in any way deformed / so as to be an unsightly or disgusting object, / or an improper person to be allowed / in or on the streets, highways, thoroughfares, / or public places in this city, / shall not therein or thereon / expose themselves to public view, / under the penalty of $1 for each offense." / Any person who looked like me / was deemed disgusting / and was locked away / from the eyes of the upstanding citizens. // I am too pretty for some Ugly Laws. / Too smooth to be shut in. / Too smart and eclectic / for any box you put me in. / My swagger is too bold / to be swept up in these public streets. // You can stare at me all you want. / No cop will buss in my head / and carry me away to an institution. / No doctor will diagnose me / a helpless invalid with an incurable disease. / No angry mob with clubs and torches / will try to run me out of town. / Whatever you do, / my roots are rigid / like a hundred-year-old tree. / I will stay right here / to glare at your ugly face too.

Ralph Savarese:

Thank you, Lateef. And now a question from the audience for D.J. "D.J., how do you imagine a productive relationship between scholars and activists as it relates to disability justice? Or more to the point: How can scholars engage in disability justice without co-opting activist work?"

D.J. Savarese:

Connect and relate with real people instead of simply creating theoretical constructs that build on words upon words. I love being both a scholar and an artful activist. And if we allow ourselves to be more than one thing we will all flourish and breathe more freely.

Ralph Savarese:

Thank you, D.J. And now here is a previously asked question by Jeremy Sicile-Kira: "D.J., please explain what you think is the first concrete step that we who have won the inclusion lottery can do to help those who haven't won. Frankly, in my mind, I greatly help others by showing them how my life as a visionary artist very much helps others, even if I don't speak at conferences anymore. I dearly feel that I am more included and accepted in the artist community than in the educational or social service systems that are there to help us truly. My disability is never a focus. Whenever my art is shown, truly, I have to say I justly believe that there is real inclusion."

D.J. Savarese:

Jeremy, thank you for your question and your artwork. Before I answer, let me say that I'd like to do away with the concepts of inclusion and the lottery. They fortify the garden wall. It's also so important not to talk about systems. Systems aren't there to help us. Maybe people working in educational or social service communities are people who nourish us, but not the systems themselves.

For example, in the film, viewers meet Mrs. Hanson, my speech and drama teacher who asked me to write and direct two readers' theaters at my high school, and Mr. Rudolph, my English teacher who engaged with me as a fellow poet and aspiring writer, and not just as a student. So, to answer your question, I'm less about saying, "Do this and then this and then this," and more about simultaneously seeding possibilities and seeing which ones grow. Throughout my life, I've had many fearless mentors. Currently, Marshall Ganz is one of them. As a community organizer, he played a major role in organizing the Montgomery bus boycott in Alabama and the National Farm Workers Association in California, but do any of you know him by name or by sight? My guess is you don't. That's because Marshall Ganz understands that "leaders aren't famous people. They are massively and resiliently hopeful people who support others in their shared goals in the face of uncertainty." I dream of being such a leader. He's shown me that relationships and webs of interdependence are a source of strength. He's taught me that my instincts are right and can change how we live, that if we work collectively, we will be wiser than if we profess to have all the answers.

Let me give you a few examples. I'm currently writing a book of poems with four other artists, three poets and one visual artist whose work we converse with in words. Originally, I intended to write the book myself, but I soon realized doing it collectively with four other artists would enrich the book, create a community—making a solitary activity more fun, especially during the pandemic—and add connections to each of our lives, connections and relationships that might grow in multiple unforeseen ways in the future. Another example is a project I'm undertaking as a board member of the Alliance for Citizen Directed Supports called Lives-in-Progress. A national collection of narratives and pathways, Lives-in-Progress is not meant to be a roadmap but, rather, a place where people can come to find the threads that interest them and begin to connect themselves rhizomatically with others.

Ralph Savarese:

Thank you. And now we have a question from the audience for Lateef. "Lateef, you mentioned something about disabled people being treated harsher, or resulting in death more often, by the police, which made me think: Do you find that ableism and racism throughout our society compound upon each other or does one seem to cancel out the other?"

Lateef McLeod:

Actually, oppressions like ableism and racism work in concert with each other and compound on each other, depending on the position of one's identity. Nirmala Erevelles talks about this in her book *Disability and Difference in Global Contexts*, explaining this. That is why disability justice has intersectionality as one of its principles.

Joel Michael Reynolds:

Hello, everyone, my name is Joel Michael Reynolds. I'm a white guy in my mid-thirties. I'm wearing a white, buttoned up T-shirt with a very boring gray blazer over it and somewhat large glasses. The first question I'd like to ask D.J. goes like this: D.J., you demonstrate how powerful the art of poetry—and specifically the unique relationship to language that poetry effects—can be for disability justice, and also to animate the hope that would carry it forward. Much of this demonstration comes, it seems, via the workings of the imagination, that curious faculty, capacity, power, ability—all those words seem wrong or at least insufficient—that might allow us to take the rhizome as our inspiration instead of true roots, or to symbolically move into the field and beyond the garden. What role do you think the imagination plays and perhaps even must play for disability justice?

D.J. Savarese:

Thank you for hearing me, Joel. Poetry does animate hope, and hoping and imagining are accelerants to new ways of being. I can say this, Joel. I am able to make myself become who I wish to become. And sometimes I do this by imagining myself and intentionally meditating until I grow into myself, but other times I have to creatively improvise around attitudinal barriers to rhize and thrive. If I have multiple directions in which I can move and grow, I can't be stopped. In my essay "Out to There," I quote Jill Magi who points out the deadening of the average true root. I can't recite it because I don't know it by heart, but she calls on those in the dominant culture, what I call the "cultivated garden," to re-enliven their senses, to reach beyond the confines of their own selves, because only there is growing possible. And she's right. She may be thinking about the environment and not of disability, but still she's right.

Now, if you're asking me, does artful activism do what laws and policies can't? The answer is yes. Artful activism awakens the senses, and I've found that art can lower people's defenses and open their eyes to new ways of both seeing and being, allowing my perceived adversaries to become my fresh-thinking allies. Art can also offer you room to create an alternative world. By trying out something new, you might creatively show people that their assumptions about you or the world we live in are unfounded. I think allowing them to make these discoveries on their own is more effective than dictating what they ought to think or feel. So, imagining is a piece of this process, but it's not all of it by my account.

Joel Michael Reynolds:

I'm next going to ask a live question from the audience for Lateef. "Neurotypical professionals and educators have often an incredibly harmful bias toward interventions that end up encouraging normalcy. How can we dismantle these therapeutic and educational systems that encourage normalcy?"

Lateef McLeod:

I think we just must get more people with disabilities in those fields to challenge the misconceptions that precedes normalcy.

And I've advised there need to be disabled consultants that enter those fields with a disabled experience who could express a different narrative.

Joel Michael Reynolds:

Lateef, another question, this one from Leroy Moore. Leroy hoped to join us by video, but that unfortunately didn't happen. Here's the question: "Being a Black disabled man, what is the work that needs to be done in the Black community on disability?"

Lateef McLeod:

The Black community in America exists in a society that is very ableist. So, it is understandable that African Americans have some misconceptions and prejudices about the disability community. However, African Americans have an opportunity to overcome their prejudices by listening and engaging with Black disabled people so we can really rise with each other and to understand how we can live and work together. Actually, I don't think African Americans are unique in this challenge, and I think these dialogues about disability politics need to take place in all communities in this country because ableism is so pervasive. I think with this dialogue and communication engagement, we can devise how we can be less ableist as a society and head toward the more disability justice future.

Joel Michael Reynolds:

Next on the schedule, we have a question from Rosemarie Garland-Thomson.

Rosemarie Garland-Thomson:

D.J., in your presentation, you offer us the metaphor of the human community as a field where a profusion of diverse forms of living things can grow into themselves and flourish as they are. This is a very inviting and ethical version of biodiversity that's largely accepted in reference to the plant and animal world. But the idea of conserving and supporting the kind of human biodiversity that people with disabilities like you and I represent seems quite counterintuitive within a medical framework that understands us as abnormal and diseased. Our human variations are very often the target of elimination rather than support and appreciation. So, my question is, how can your metaphor of a field where human diversity can flourish be brought to the medical science communities that define our diversity as disease that compromises life quality for us and for the human community?

D.J. Savarese:

Rosemarie, allow me to begin by thanking you for your pioneering work in the field of disability studies. I have a lot of different responses to this question. If I am ever to bring change to the world, I need to simply refuse to accept assumptions as facts. I believe if we want to move beyond the medical and social constructivist models of disability, we need to stop addressing them directly. I don't think we make change by engaging with a medical model per se, but I do think we can make change when we connect with people within the medical science community. Can I say why?

I have screened *Deej* at some medical universities and found that it elicited fresh thinking. And my work is closely followed by a number of medical professionals, some of whom are parents, siblings, grandparents, aunts, or uncles of a nonspeaking or neurodivergent person, and some of whom are not. I like to think that *Deej* takes them away from the medical versus social constructivist argument and into the field of sensory sensation. I remember I was scared to present at the Indiana University Medical School. I thought that every question would be about my difference as debilitating—but, in fact, the first person to speak was the head of the medical school. Rather than ask a question, he made this comment: "I envy you, D.J. The fresh air never sings to my lungs. My sensory experience is nowhere near as vibrant as yours. I came here prepared to pity you, but I leave here pitying myself and my truncated awareness of the world around me."

Likewise, my psychiatrist of eighteen years often seeks out my counsel about patients who aren't able to communicate. He knows he doesn't know, and he's willing to ask me for help. And at UPenn, after a film screening, neuroscience majors witnessed my interactions with a young AAC user and his parents. They began to see how we break out of the textbook molds they've been offered. And I think each relationship, each of these experiences, plants innumerable seeds for the next generations. These connections ignore the garden wall, the medical constructs that try to confine us and fail.

Joel Michael Reynolds:

And now I'd like to ask another live question for Lateef, and the question goes like this: "Can artful activism be learned and practiced within the confines of systems to broaden, disrupt, and ultimately improve or render such systems obsolete? Or," the questioner asked, "am I simply thinking too linearly?"

Lateef McLeod:

Well, since our collective wisdom had to be taught by disabled people, and we have yet to systematically promote disabled thought so it's widely known or taught, I think we have to do the work of systematized thinking of this knowledge. This way it becomes widely available, and more people will be educated by it.

Johnson Cheu:

Hey, everyone. It's Johnson Cheu. I'm sorry I couldn't be with you. It's finals week here, so lots of things to do. Anyway, your paper chronicles your thoughts on barriers to inclusive society more generally and to disability arts in particular. So, my question concerns allies and inclusion. As specific examples for context, the head writer of *A Million Little Things* wanted to include some of his real-life experiences with his physically disabled brother on air in that show. And there's also the recently revealed revelation that some of the producers and writers on that television show, among other things, have parents with disabilities. And that was the impetus for their current storyline with a paralyzed character. We don't know whether the paralysis will be temporary or permanent, played by able-bodied actor David Giuntoli. So, my question is how to include allies in the disability rights movement and then how to help ensure that the disability portrayals still maintain an air of authenticity. Thank you.

Lateef McLeod:

Yes, allies in the disability movement are very important. From my experience, people do not really think about disability unless they have a personal experience with it, either by having a disability or having a relationship with someone with a disability. Allies of the disability community who are in positions of power can promote disability issues and have the ability to promote our culture and to have a more disability justice mindset. The disability community should work with these allies so that a disability-liberated world will come into fruition.

Joel Michael Reynolds:

And finally, for our exchange with the live audience, we have one more question for D.J. "D.J., you have a background in anthropology. Do you have examples of international disability liberation movements from studying places outside of the United States?"

D.J. Savarese:

I don't really have examples of disability liberation internationally, but I came to love anthropology for its privileging of the insider's perspective and its insistence that we self-reflect on our own cultural assumptions as well. It also gave me a true sense of self-identity to have a professor, advisor, and mentor who studies the Nepali Deaf culture as a culture with its own language and not as a disabled population. Anthropology also very much informed my understanding of self-representation during the making of the film.

Joel Michael Reynolds:

One more question from the audience. "D.J., your poetic words about rhizomes, the garden wall, and ecology very strikingly remind the audience of the relationship between humans and nature. Could you say more about how you think about the ties between the liberation of humans and the liberation of animals and nature, especially when it comes to combating implicit bias?"

D.J. Savarese:

Thank you for your questions. I think we liberate ourselves when we learn from the resilience and creative improvising of the natural world and when we humbly take our place in our shared ecosystem. I hope science curricula will change to engage each of us in being mindful and connected with our fellow beings within our ecosystem, rather than seeing us as the managers at the top of some hierarchical pyramid.

Rosemarie Garland-Thomson:

Yes, thank you. And thank you, everyone, for this really wonderful presentation, this project, this gathering. Many of us have transitioned from primarily in-person environments and forms of communication with one another over the last months, and it's been interesting to observe how using this particular format that we're using here, the virtual gathering, the Zoom format, has highlighted something that is really important about culture, work, and education: which is that more and more people with disabilities are coming together.

And that coming together to make knowledge, to work, or to be in the educational world contrasts with past experiences in a work setting where we're the only people with disabilities there. And then we need to ask for accommodation; we need to arrange an accessible environment, and it becomes tedious and difficult to do that. It is so exciting here to think about how so many of us are gathered together just in this little project with different access technologies, different ways of being together. I was struck by how I, and also Lateef and D.J., need to use a Zoom environment like this. So, because I don't type, because I don't keyboard, I use my voice. I use my mouth more than I use my hands. And it's fascinating to watch how we all are adjusting to one another's needs. So, I want to say, in terms of clapping, Erik just requested that we might want to clap or snap our fingers in appreciation. I don't snap my fingers, and I don't clap, but I have adopted a way of clapping or a way of applauding from the Deaf culture. And that is to do this. [She moves one hand vigorously back and forth]. This, my dears, is the sound of one hand clapping. So, I want to say yay for everybody. You are wonderful; thank you for all of the work that you all do.

4

Questioning Cure

Disability, Identity, and Healing

Anand Prahlad, Ann Millett-Gallant, and Karen Nakamura

Liz Bowen:

Hello everyone, and welcome to "Questioning Cure: Disability, Identity, and Healing." My name is Liz Bowen, and I'm the Rice Family Fellow in Bioethics and the Humanities at The Hastings Center. I am the associate director of *The Art of Flourishing: Conversations on Disability* series, along with my co-organizers Erik Parens, Joel Michael Reynolds, and Rosemarie Garland-Thomson.

With that, I will turn it over to my colleague Erik Parens, senior research scholar at The Hastings Center and Director of the National Endowment for the Humanities-funded Initiative on Bioethics and the Humanities.

Erik Parens:

Thanks to all of you for joining this fourth event in our series, *The Art of Flourishing: Conversations on Disability.*

Since its inception in 1969, scholars at The Hastings Center have critiqued the institution of medicine. One of the Center's Founding Fellows, Eric Cassell, argued that a fundamental problem with medicine is that it too often harbors a reductive, mechanistic conception of human beings. Cassell thought that if physicians were truly to become *healers*, they would need a deeper, richer, more holistic conception of human beings.

Rather than view patients first as *bodies* that are in pain and need fixing or *cure*, Cassell thought patients needed to be viewed as *persons* who have experiences and need *care*. He argued that, to make the transition from being glorified mechanics to being healers, physicians needed to *listen* to patients—and to take them at their word when they reported what their experiences were like for them.

This bioethical critique of medicine emerged in the same historical moment when people with disabilities began organizing to demand that their experiences be listened to. That is, the bioethical critique of the institution of medicine arose around the same time as the disability critique of the "medical model" of disability. As everyone here today knows very well, according to the disability critique, most of the problems that disabled people experience are rooted not in the brokenness or atypicality of individual bodies, but in the unjust, unaccommodating structure of our society.

My point is that Hastings-style bioethicists and disability theorists and activists have a shared commitment to "questioning cure." It is not that any of us is, in principle, *against* cure. It is that we are *for* distinguishing between real cures, on the one hand, and poisons that masquerade as cures, on the other. We are *for* remembering that when real cures are not possible or desired, healing still can be possible. And we are *for* remembering that the tools that the institution of medicine can offer are often *not* the tools that disabled people need to promote their own flourishing.

Our first speaker is Anand Prahlad, who is professor emeritus in the Department of English at the University of Missouri. He is a folklorist, disability activist, musician, and author of the memoir *The Secret Life of a Black Aspie*. Prahlad will suggest that in a society that is racist, to be Black is to be traumatized and to be disabled. Analogously, in a society that is based on neurotypicality, to be autistic is to be disabled. According to Prahlad, the same ableist society that creates those disabilities also manufactures a "cure" that is, in fact, a poison. The poisonous "cure" is either to conform to norms of whiteness and neurotypicality, or to disappear. Rejecting that poisonous "cure," Prahlad will prescribe what we might call genuine healing.

Our second speaker, Ann Millett-Gallant, is an art historian and disability studies scholar who teaches at the University of North Carolina at Greensboro and is the author of the memoir *Re-Membering: Putting Mind and Body Back Together Following Traumatic Brain Injury*. In 2007, Ann suffered a traumatic brain injury (TBI). In her remarks, she will use the term cure, without scare quotes, and she will suggest how even a true cure is importantly different from healing. While Ann would have welcomed being cured of some of the distressing symptoms that resulted from her TBI, cure of those symptoms was not possible. But what was possible was to heal. As Ann will explain, it was possible for her, enmeshed in her community and engaged in her art, to flourish in her own new way.

Our third speaker, Karen Nakamura, is a cultural and visual anthropologist at the University of California, Berkeley. She will speak about the way in which the idea of cure is often wholly irrelevant to someone's ability to flourish. Rather than needing any sort of cure, Karen will speak about disabled people needing tools—tools for hacking environments that weren't built for atypical bodies. Again, it is not atypical bodies that need to change, but unsupportive environments that need to change.

After our three speakers have offered their remarks, Rosemarie Garland-Thomson will facilitate a brief conversation among them, and for the remainder of the event, Joel Reynolds will facilitate the conversation with all of you in the audience. It is now my pleasure to turn the mic over to Prahlad.

Anand Prahlad:

Thank you, Erik, for that introduction. I am in a Black man's body. I am dark-skinned. I have on a hat that my dreadlocks are tucked under. And I'm against the background of an orange wall that has some white paint at the bottom.

I'll begin by talking briefly about my disabilities to put the rest of my comments into perspective. All of my disabilities have been socially imagined or politically engineered by white American institutions. My first disability in American society is my Blackness, for since the fifteenth-century incursion of Europeans into Africa and the subsequent slave trade, Blackness in the white imagination has been constructed as both a physical deformity and a mental impairment. So racism is a widely unacknowledged form of ableism.

My second disability is PTSS—post-traumatic slave syndrome—and intergenerational trauma that affects most people of African descent in the Western Hemisphere. My third disability is my own PTSD—trauma from the ongoing racial abuse in my own lifetime.

The fourth disability I mention here is my autism. Like many from my background, I think of the idea of curing disabilities as a fairytale, spun by white institutions and sold to the masses. It's like the tale of the ugly beast that kisses a beautiful princess and is suddenly transformed into a handsome prince. It exploits people's suffering and offers them false promises. It invites us to think of disability as an individual issue and distracts us from focusing on collective and systemic problems. It translates into fixing us, which means making us into something that conforms to our white so-called normal.

Cure is much more about culture than it is about medicine and health. Meanwhile, some of us are so different that society declares us unredeemable, too broken to be fixed, too different to ever become anything close to the white normal. For us, the recommended cure is more explicitly exile, genocide, or eugenics. The actual goal, then, is to cure society of us more than it is to treat what ails our minds, spirits, or bodies.

I remember as a child growing up in rural Virginia, a stone's throw from the plantation where my ancestors were slaves, in the age of segregation. We had little access to healthcare other than natural remedies. We were exiled from white society except as house cleaners, nannies, or manual laborers. We were disposable. And meanwhile, in the nearby medical hospitals, scientists and doctors were busy experimenting on Black bodies of men, women, and children. We were being used like lab rats, to experiment and develop medicines and treatments that would ironically be denied to those like us.

While many things have changed since segregation officially ended, many things have not. I dare say that for large percentages of Black disabled people, perhaps for disabled people in general, being able to truly flourish is still as elusive as it ever was. Under slavery, able-bodied and disabled Black people found ways to subvert the system, to take care of themselves as best they could, to maintain positive self-identities. And we have continued to do so. But in the end, the enslaved were still enslaved, and in many fundamental ways, our modern lives are still shaped by similar forms of oppression.

The system we live in is brutal, inhumane, and sadistic, and it values money, things, and "winners" above human dignity and well-being. It perpetuates the most superficial ideas of beauty and dismisses any profound concern with developing the inner life. Still, we survive. We subvert. We sometimes achieve and excel. But how often do we truly flourish?

To use myself as an example, I have been able to have a career and families, and to be fairly successful as an author and scholar. But in my sixty-seven years on planet Earth, I have never had a day where I felt safe; where I was not afraid or anxious; where I was not looking over my shoulder; where I was not reeling from a combination of transgenerational and present-day trauma; and where I was not on the edge of losing my fragile grip on my ability to function socially and end up either institutionalized, homeless, or otherwise removed from society.

Every day I have felt viscerally my health deteriorating as a result of the stigmas attached to my disabilities. It is well documented that environmental racism, a form of ableism, is a leading cause of physical and mental illness among Black people, as well as a major reason for our short life expectancies. This also holds true for many other forms of disability. I've had moments in which I flourish, certainly, but as I weigh those against the days and months and years of mental and emotional distress or debilitating physical pain, I am more saddened than uplifted.

It is not enough for us to think in terms of just surviving or stealing pieces of dignity here and there. I believe that dignity, care, and the right to flourish should be guaranteed for everyone, not for occasional moments or as goals we have to wage endless battles for, but as givens from the moment of birth to the moment when we exit this plane of existence.

We no longer have the luxury of time to wait for a change. If the system isn't radically transformed, and soon, we will all be facing economic and social collapse that will lead to unprecedented and widespread suffering and despair. And as always, those of us who are the most vulnerable will suffer the most and be considered the most expendable.

Despite the enormity of injustices like the pandemic and environmental racism, we need to be actively imagining a different kind of society and a different kind of world, one in which community and understanding connections with each other and nature are the rules, not the exceptions. To do this, we will have to throw away the book of capitalist fairytales and create new stories that reflect a different vision.

The titles we have been raised on tell us that human beings are strong. They can do amazing things with their minds and bodies, withstand impossible conditions, and conquer any obstacle. The truth is actually a little different, though. Human beings are incredibly fragile. They break easily. They have a difficult time facing problems. They tend to elevate physical and technological achievements above quality of being. We need to create stories in which the most important achievements are those that happen inside our hearts, spirits, and minds.

The old stories have also taught us to think of people as individuals. We have the "self-made man" and "pulling ourselves up from our bootstraps." But this is also a kind of fairy tale. If I can use myself again as an example: as an autistic person with synesthesia, not only having my senses overlap but also having physical empathy, I have never felt the sense of "I-ness" that I understand is considered "normal." My "I" has always included those around me, but also the natural world, for example, birds and trees. I am the cardinal that sings outside my window in the morning. Not metaphorically, but really. And the cardinal is me.

It's one of the reasons why I can't imagine flourishing as an individual thing. How can I flourish if all the "me"s aren't? How can I flourish if my brothers and sisters are in pain or are dying? If the bees and butterflies that are a part of me are dying? And so our new stories have to reflect the interconnectedness between all forms to impart the idea that all of our well-being depends on the well-being of all.

In the end, it is society that really needs to be cured—the society in which, for example, sadistic personality disorders and delusional disorders among those in power are considered normal, even admired; the society in which all too many have fallen under the spell of ableist fairy tales that malign all but the narrowest ideas of beauty; the society in which we rationalize the bullying of those who are different and celebrate the most superficial notions of what it means to be human. For now, those of us who are, in society's eyes, different will continue to find ways to inscribe our realities in the public consciousness, to fight for a change, and to envision a society and world in which fundamental healing becomes more of a focus than cure.

Liz Bowen:

Thank you, Prahlad. We are going to move along to Ann Millett-Gallant next.

Ann Millett-Gallant:

My identity as disabled is multifaceted. My medical diagnosis at birth was congenital amputation of all four limbs, suggesting I lacked arms and legs. Such terminology points to what is assumed missing or what has been lost, rather than describing my asymmetrical physique. My limbs never developed in my mother's womb fully but grew into identifiable and usable amputee shapes. My family, friends, and most of my communities taught and encouraged me to feel and function as "complete."

I am further privileged as a white academic. I hold a PhD in art history and publish my research on representations of disability in art and visual culture. I have strong support systems and adequate financial resources. Others have complimented my adaptability and, for the most part, positive attitude. I am/was someone whom others assumed knew myself well, and I saw myself as shining a bright light on all my projects.

In mid-2007, I was vacationing with a good friend, Anna, in San Francisco, and at the end of a rigorous day of sightseeing, I lost control of the travel scooter I was driving. I tipped over the curb and came crashing down on the left side of my body and head, intensely. I lost consciousness. Luckily, I have been told, this happened close to a prominent trauma center. Anna later told me that someone at this hospital told her that had I been taken elsewhere, no one would have tried to save me, likely.

Other notes my father wrote revealed that when I arrived at the hospital, I was within twenty minutes of dying. He also noted his frustrations that no one was allowed to ask questions. I have read that physicians refuse to make any predictions about the results of traumatic brain injury (TBI), characteristically, because of the diverseness of the effects, not to mention the inconceivability for most people of the trauma. After impact, I was comatose for six weeks, followed by alternating states of revival and unconsciousness. Somewhere or somehow, I decided to survive. I was accomplished already, and I wasn't finished.

As I regained cognizance and strength, my future was discussed without me, but consensus led me home. I traveled from San Francisco to Columbus, Ohio, in June 2007. I lived with and relied primarily on my mother, who was the first person to reach me in California. Her continued presence and energy brought feelings of security, comfort, and hope. I had many resources already in Ohio, and because I was practically uninsured after completing my PhD degree, my father liquidated my savings and investments totally so I could qualify for Medicaid disability insurance. A journalist published a story about me in the *Columbus Dispatch*, titled "Willpower," that features a large close-up of my face, wearing makeup and earrings to offset that I had lost part of my skull. In 2010, I found it and felt startled. I recognized myself as a deer caught in headlights (Figure 4.1). I recreated the photograph as a drawing with earrings and white-out placed specifically at the side of my brain trauma to emphasize my eyes and accentuate my humanity. *Self-Portrait with Hemicraniectomy* is a black-and-white drawing of my face looking straight ahead with short, cropped hair.

My brain and my body have fought many battles together. I returned to live in Durham, North Carolina, at the end of 2007. I began teaching a course for the Bachelor of Arts in Liberal & Interdisciplinary Studies Program for the University of North Carolina at Greensboro and was working full-time by the fall semester of 2008. I healed gradually over several years through intense physical therapy and art therapy sessions. I emphasize the term "healed," rather than "cured." This distinction is crucial. After being fitted for prosthetic legs, twice, while suffering unbearable muscle spasms, lack of sleep, increased anxiety, and an unexplainable bone infection, I decided to forgo the prosthetics and be comfortable in my own skin.

In synthesis, the goals of art therapy are to heal rather than to cure. Scholars and practitioners assert that trauma cannot be expressed in words due to its complexity and personalized nature.[1] Painting, drawing, and collaging imagery, storytelling,

Figure 4.1 *Self-Portrait with Hemicraniectomy*, ink on paper, 11 × 8.5 in (2009)

and analyzing my artwork with a therapist did not erase my traumatic past, but rather helped me regain memories, cope with new impairments, and refashion my body images. In 2017, I wrote a memoir, composed with years of journaling, notes from my family, my medical records, research on TBI and art therapy, and examples of my artwork.[2] Neurologist Rudi Coetzer states that anxiety and depression are the most typical results of TBI and that feeling guilty constantly signals depression.[3] By juxtaposing pictures that spoke to me about my ongoing side effects, losses of self-confidence, and persistent guilt, I healed many wounds. Collages helped crystallize my memory and synthesize my past and present experiences. Creative projects prove to be therapeutic still. Over time, I have become more confident and resilient.

For today, I collaged three printed images of my paintings from the past 11 years, by adhering them to a canvas painted orange and with three accompanying words—"Trauma," "Drama," and "Mama"—drawn below them (Figure 4.2). My depiction of an inside/outside view of my brain after it was severed is left-justified. An exterior depiction of my cranium with the image of a red cabbage

Figure 4.2 *Trauma, Drama, Mama*, mixed media on canvas, 11 × 14 in (2021)

cut in half, whose intricate, painted ridges resemble the inside of my brain, rests on top of it.

"Cabbage" is an offensive term that chastises people who are not "normal." Sometimes stigma takes the form of questions like, "What happened to you?" and "How long have you been doing things for yourself?" Sometimes, others' analysis of my experiences, in terms such as, "You are just like how everyone loses their minds as they age," make me defensive and irritated. Sometimes I turn these interactions into teachable moments. Other times I reply, "No," and often, in varying tones, just say, "Born this way." Contrasting with others' deadpan assertions, my cabbage is bejeweled and adorned with a ghoulish dancing center. In hues of rose and grape, this tactile shell pumps with life.

Next to the vibrant *Cabbage* is a mixed-media painting, *Ann's Beautiful Broken Brain*, inspired by my perceptions of the documentary film, *My Beautiful Broken Brain*.[4] This image of two shapes in blue hues floating on a rosy background includes, at the left, a cat, and at the right, a brain and face depicted abstractly. I sketched from brain scans and incorporated, as my eyes, the signature swirl I crafted through art therapy and that I envisioned rotating outward to relieve my anxiety and the lingering muscle contraction in my one wounded knee. The third image of my artwork, picturing my fluffy tabby cat, Waffles, is right-justified. This tactile interaction between a twisting cat and my left, rounded hand references my role as "mama" to cats and my relationships with other loved ones.

Craft paper with rosy polka dots frames the three images, adding elements of whimsy and delight. These borders overlap for me, cerebrally and somatically. Spelled out in a hybrid font with more swirls are three titles for the compositions: *Trauma, Drama, Mama*. These terms rhyme and provide names for my roles in life. The collage stages three personal images, or "self-portraits," and links them to articulate multidimensional journeys. This trio references self-care, care, and interdependence. I will never be "cured," but now I have the tools I need to feel "healed."

Karen Nakamura:

Hi, everyone. It's delightful to see you today. Thank you for coming. I'm really honored to be here. Today I would like to talk about what I see as the crip's dilemma: whether we cure ourself or hack the world. The cure industry says, "Why are disabled people so hesitant about the cure?" Perhaps because it always seems to invoke other "C"s: control, compliance, conformity.

We can perhaps see this most aptly in psychopharmaceuticals used to control people with psychiatric disabilities such as myself. The taking of these drugs is often not within our control. We are often forced into compliance, monitored for compliance, and the goal of the drug "therapy" is conformity to social standards rather than any alleviation of our own pain.

But we can see this in other domains as well. Think of the cochlear implantation of two-year-olds. Here again, control, compliance, and conformity are operant, not only in the implantation of the cochlear implant, but also in the postimplantation speech therapy protocols, as chronicled by Laura Mauldin in *Made to Hear*. Signing is forbidden. The child must comply to hearing conformity.

To take the cure, we have to accept the control of normative medicine, and be compliant and conform. Is this really too much to ask? Ultimately, in the end, most of us learn that the way of the cure is futile. Now whatever we do to try to conform, we will always stick out, always be the other.

Crip scholar Alison Kafer talks about the forestalled nature of "crip futurities"; the cure is always presented as being just over the hill: six months, two years, ten years. If we could just be patient and wait for it, we might find it. I think we've been "patient" and been "patients" for too long, and we know the false promises of the cure. We can wait, but it will never come.

We were always already human and posthuman. In the social sciences and humanities these days, it's fashionable to talk about the turn toward "posthumanism"—that is, tearing down the divide between the "human" and "nonhuman"—whether it be to talk about cyborg bodies or the symbiosis of our microbiomes. However, crips have always known that we were always already human and posthuman.

In 1995, two months after his friend's death, Mike Boyd dropped off Ed Roberts's wheelchair on the doorstep at the Smithsonian "castle" in Washington, DC. Ed's chair revealed the marks and dents of the many battles this disability activist fought for his own civil rights and those of others.

At the Smithsonian, it became part of the national collection along with other artifacts, including George Washington's dentures. And I like to think that the comparison is fitting. Ed's chair was very much part of his body, like George's teeth. And like George's teeth, Ed's chair was designed to be part of his body. It had a portable respirator, a portable ramp in the days before curb cuts, straps to keep his upper body stabilized, and a joystick positioned in just the right position. Anyone else sitting in Ed's chair would feel like they had George's teeth in their mouth.

Every disabled person is an engineer. This is the philosophy undergirding the website "Engineering at Home," headed by Sara Hendren and Caitrin Lynch. It chronicles the household applications created by Cindy, who had a quadruple amputation following a medical emergency. The adaptations are mundane— a way to pour out laundry detergent, a hand clasp for a stick of deodorant—but they are also innovative and creative.

Hendren and Lynch's point is that we are all engineers and designers, and disabled people particularly so, given that the world is not designed for us and our needs. Every day, we have to engage in hacks: using our canes to operate elevator buttons, putting tactile dots on our appliances to know where the buttons are, letting our service dogs carry our medications so that they can remind us to take them.

Architect Jonah Keller and crip scholar Margaret Price have written about how disabled people hack spaces, making use of buildings and our built environment in ways that the (able-bodied, neurotypical) designer perhaps never imagined. We find the hidden light switches, the quiet nooks, the clear sightlines, the service entrances, the doors that aren't locked, and the underground paths. We convene and create crip space by our very presence.

Gallaudet University is the world's only four-year college for Deaf and hard-of-hearing students. Nestled in southeast Washington, DC, its campus was originally designed by Frederick Law Olmsted in 1866. Not to insult it or him, but it looks like almost every other college campus in the Northeast. At a time when it was important to stress that Deaf students could attend college, it was important for Gallaudet to express this sense of normality. But by the end of the twentieth century, times have changed. In 1988, the Deaf President Now (DPN) movement had instilled a Deaf man as the first president of Gallaudet. In 1990, the Americans with Disabilities Act had ensured everyone could go to college.

More quietly, though, in the background, deafness had become partly cured. The 1988 Deaf President Now movement had been caused in part by the epidemiological and demographic bubble of deaf kids created by a rubella epidemic in the 1960s. The measles, mumps, and rubella (MMR) vaccine would ensure that there would be no more future demographic bubbles. Genetic counseling, which Gallaudet itself offers, would reduce genetic causes, and cochlear implant technology could take care of much of the rest. Gallaudet would face a future shrinking population of students.

In 2005, architect Hansel Bauman and a cohort of fiery deaf scholars at Gallaudet created the DeafSpace project. Its goal was to fundamentally change how buildings and spaces at Gallaudet were designed and created. They made a manifesto about how signing deaf people occupy space and used it to change the hallways. Common spaces, elevators, stairs, slopes, paths, classrooms, offices, and even walls were designed and created.

I've talked about the difference between curing and hacking space. But what of mad activists? As a mad activist and scholar,

I wonder how this cure/hacking dilemma applies to us. We have a much more troubled relation with biomedicine than some of our physically or intellectually disabled kin.

In my more fiery days, I was fairly anti-pharma. I refused to take the pills that were literally poison. But the world is equally toxic, and fighting the world constantly is equally draining. And psycho-pharma does make it easier to just live. And that's our dilemma. We don't have adequate metaphors for what the little "pill" means for us. Is it just compliance, conformity, control? Or are they perhaps also the wheelchairs and canes that let us navigate the world around us and make it tolerable for us? How can we mad activists work to rework the built environment and social institutions so that we don't have to constantly take this false cure? We're still very much at the beginning of our movement, and I have few answers.

As an anthropologist, I often wonder if archeologists a thousand or ten thousand years from now will know we existed. And by "we," I mean "disabled people." My friend and crip artist Riva Lehrer talks about going to a museum and recognizing one of the skeletons on display as having the same type of scoliosis as her. She imagined the life that this person might have had. Sometimes our disabilities are visible on our bodies. But what about the artifacts we leave behind? The new Gallaudet that is being redesigned as DeafSpace will certainly be visible if the archeologists know what to look for. What about other spaces?

Bryan Bashin, the head of the San Francisco LightHouse for the Blind and Visually Impaired, tells a wonderful story of going to the home of a mysterious benefactor who left S.F. LightHouse $125 million. He instantly recognized the home as that of a person who is slowly going blind: the tactile art, the magnifying glasses, the bright lamps, the large television screens placed in odd spaces. Will these types of details be apparent to our future archeologists? Or only maybe if they were blind, would they realize them?

I wonder what the traces we leave behind will be. And so I exhort to you, my invisible audience behind the Zoom screen, reject the cure. Try to hack your spaces. Hack your world. Leave traces behind. Be remembered. Thank you.

Rosemarie Garland-Thomson:

Thank you very much for these three wonderful presentations, Prahlad, Ann, and Karen. I have a few questions that are prompts for discussion among the three panelists, so I invite you all to participate together in a conversation.

The first question that I wanted to put forward is this one: People with disabilities who have managed to flourish and to live lives that most of us would consider to be good are often described as being "strong." I was struck by the contrast between this stereotype of "strong" disabled people and Prahlad's point, which seems to me to be very true, which is that human beings are incredibly fragile. How can we talk about flourishing as we have experienced it in our own lives? How can we understand that in relation to this fact of human fragility? Anyone want to begin?

Anand Prahlad:

When I think of strength, and when I'm talking about strength, I'm referencing the way people tend to think of strength and what they tend to think of as "strong." For example, you are strong if you can lift five hundred pounds, or you are strong if you can endure a certain amount of pain, or you are strong if you cannot show your emotions. So as I'm thinking about it and talking about it, I'm trying to suggest taking on strength in a different way. Our bodies are fragile. We don't have fur. If you dropped us off at the North Pole naked, we would die. We are so susceptible to so many things—environmentally, in nature—and it doesn't take a lot to cause harm to a human body or a human mind or human spirit. In some cases, it takes very little. So that's sort of what I mean when I say we are fragile. I'm suggesting we think of strength in different ways than it is typically thought of. For example, it takes strength to try to understand yourself. It takes strength to look at your fear. Those kinds of things are what I'm suggesting would be a more meaningful way to think about being strong than the typical ways that people often think about it.

Ann Millett-Gallant:

I think that people always say, "You are so strong because you have overcome so many things." And I have overcome certain things, like environments that don't accommodate me, or structures that don't address me properly, or doctors that haven't treated me. But we are mortal, and we are sensitive, and we wound, and we get hurt physically and emotionally. And the idea of cures is the idea of a transformation from ill or disabled to nondisabled and healthy. And to see it more as, we're all on a continuum, and we all have things to deal with, and we can heal sometimes ourselves and sometimes other people. But this idea of erasing trauma from your life isn't possible. Nor is it possible to just ignore it, the trauma that we all go through. And it is always hard to go to therapy. I chose art therapy because I liked art, and I was an artist. And so some of the ways of dealing with some of our pain might be through different ways other than just medicine or typical exercises or whatever is prescribed.

Karen Nakamura:

I think when people talk about being strong, it's often in the context of, "Oh wow, you must have had some internal strength to survive the challenges that were presented to you." But from my perspective, I live with a great deal of survivor's guilt because I know many more people who are more talented and much stronger, and they didn't survive. And it was more luck than anything inherent in myself that has allowed me to come to this point, so I don't like the language of our strength because it implies there's something inherent about that. It's more that a whole bunch of us walked past this giant minefield, and a great number of us got decimated. Does that mean that there is anything special about those who didn't? No. And it is society that has created that minefield, right? It's created an environment that makes it so hard for us to exist. And by praising the survivors, you think, "Oh, that's so great, you crossed that minefield like no one." It's like, you could have not put that minefield there. You could have made it so that all of my community got across.

Anand Prahlad:

I'm going to say amen to that.

Rosemarie Garland-Thomson:

I think all of your presentations put forward the need for what I call a sustainable or a sustaining environment for all human beings to live in. But for people with disabilities, that sustaining environment requires perhaps more distinctive tools, to use Karen's concept, but tools in the very broadest sense. The kind of tools that might be technologies, the kind of tools that might be—and I think Prahlad was suggesting this—other people and other living beings, and for Ann, the kinds of tools that consist of the implements of making art. These tools are all part of the larger sustaining environment that has allowed those of us who have flourished to flourish.

So I want to suggest taking our conversation in another direction. The presentations here that the three of you offered to us affirm that it is less us, our bodies, and our minds that need to be cured, but rather that society needs to be cured. And I think Karen's concept of control, compliance, and conformity—that lovely alliterative idea—is really crucial here about curing society rather than curing us, our bodies, and our minds. Could each of you talk a little bit more about what elements of society need to be cured in order for us to flourish more effectively in the world we live in?

Karen Nakamura:

When I was teaching two years ago, disabled students would constantly say that one of the hardest things—especially in the community of people who have low energy, we call ourselves the "spoonie" community—it's often very hard to get to class. And people have been begging for years and years, "Why can't we have a Zoom option? Why doesn't all this technology make it easier?" And always, the answer was, "Oh no, we couldn't possibly do that. Oh no, it'd be impossible." And then suddenly a global pandemic hits, and it's like, "Hey, everyone can now do Zoom." And you know, suddenly all of these possibilities open up and everyone's talking about going back to the old ways: "Hey, we're really looking forward to in-person meetings, we are really looking forward to in-person classes." And for sure there are some people for whom that is the more accessible option. But we've already seen a bit of the possibilities. You know, I find Zoom very tiring, especially speaking on Zoom, where I have to have the video up. I do like Zoom meetings where everyone's on chat and it really isn't Zoom, but more like Twitter. But we have now seen some possibilities that society can change, but it only changes when it affects the majority of people. But now we can see it's possible. I think there's room.

Ann Millett-Gallant:

A lot of the access needs are still medicalized. We have to go see all kinds of different specialists to get a new wheelchair. That's an inconvenience to me. And if I have to renew my disability license plate, I have to do a lot of paperwork, and mail this, and fax that, and so on. So a lot of these things turn into a huge hassle. Also, travel has gotten even harder. It's so rushed, and people are so packed in together, and that makes it difficult. There are a lot of things with access that are difficult. There isn't one solution that is going to be accessible for all people, I suppose.

Rosemarie Garland-Thomson:

So you're suggesting that society can be cured by a different distribution of resources? I think we're all saying that. And a different set of priorities about how we build, literally, and fund the world that we share together.

Karen Nakamura:

One of my goals in teaching, and one of the reasons I like teaching large classes, is because I know I'll get at least a few students who will go on to change the world, who maybe have the resources and the privilege. But I want to at least sensitize them to start thinking about these things. And maybe I'll also have a few crips who will do it too. I think as we start to occupy more positions, maybe we'll start to have drugs that aren't toxic and don't shorten our lifespan at the cost of being able to exist. Maybe we'll have more devices. Maybe we'll have someone in an insurance company who will have the brilliant idea that maybe someone needs more than one wheelchair at a time, so you don't have to get rid of your old chair when you get a new one. Or maybe someone will design a wheelchair that will work in the rain, a power chair. I mean, there are all of these innovative thoughts, but we need to be in those positions to do that.

Rosemarie Garland-Thomson:

One of the terms that Erik offered us in his introduction is the idea of genuine healing, which I think is a really productive concept. How would any of you describe genuine healing? It seems to me that it's going to require understanding people with disabilities and illnesses as much more than our diagnostic categories, which I think we've all been talking about. To be seen more as whole people rather than broken people—that really difficult metaphor of broken and fixed. To be seen—and this seems very important in what all three of you said, and it certainly is in my own work—as people with dignity that others in the world can recognize. It seems to me that the kind of dignity that we, as people with disabilities, tried to describe in our own work and tried to elicit is a particular kind of dignity that asks to be recognized in distinctive ways. And I wondered if all of you might have something to say about what this genuine healing might be like in your world.

Anand Prahlad:

I'm also flashing back to the previous two conversations when I didn't really say anything because I didn't know what I thought. But this helps me to figure out what I'm actually thinking. I have a hard time thinking of the issues you're mentioning in isolation from the society in general. So I was thinking, "What kind of technology or tool would help an autistic person to function better in the world?" There are some things that I could think of, but while those tools might serve a few autistic people, you would still have a society that was full of intolerant, insensitive people who weren't willing to grant an autistic person dignity or space or to think of them with the same consideration that they would with someone who was not autistic.

If I'm that person, and I have to go to work every day, and on my job I have a tool—let's say I have a quiet room that I can go to—well, when I go to the grocery store, there's no quiet room. When I go anywhere else, there's no quiet room. And so I'm still living in a society where if I leave my home, I'm the subject of microaggressions and certain forms of abuse. For me, it comes back to a more holistic answer to those questions than just what technology or environment might help me. I can go walking in the woods because I'm fortunate enough to live in a place where I can go walking in the woods and where there are woods. But an autistic person living in an inner city, let's say in an impoverished neighborhood, they can't go walking in the woods. And in fact, if that person is Black, if they go walking at all, they could get shot.

So when you ask the question, How would I imagine healing taking place for me? The first thing that comes to my mind would be to cure all those people out there, and that would allow me the space to actually focus on my own healing rather than using all of my energy just to cope with a hostile environment. I could go to a retreat, but I can't live at a retreat.

Karen Nakamura:

One of my friends—a disability activist in Japan, Shunji Kadota—said he works to envision a world in which, when a child is born who is disabled, instead of everyone pitying the parents, the friends of the parents say, "That is absolutely incredible. You are so fortunate to have given birth to a disabled child because we know that that child is going to change the world." And in some ways, isn't that what all parents want? A child who will make the world a better place? And he said, "We disabled people do that. We make the world a better place. Where we go, things magically happen." Wheelchair ramps get built, automatic door openers get installed, quiet rooms at conferences get made, visible fire alarms get installed, closed captions appear on television.

All of the activism that we've done over the past sixty years has made the world a better place. And I think we need to acknowledge, and we need able-bodied, neurotypical people to acknowledge, that we are the ones that bring these changes into society, so that again, when a disabled person is born into the world, we celebrate that as the marvelous occasion for someone who has that potential for change.

Rosemarie Garland-Thomson:

Karen, thank you. You just offered the best hack that I've thought of or heard in a long time, and that is that you just hacked a gender reveal party to bring the idea of a disability reveal party, which would be exactly what you just described. People could start making cakes and all sorts of technological apparatuses to celebrate. Thank you so much. We can move on now to the next part of the program.

Joel Michael Reynolds:

We are now moving on to the section of this event that takes questions from the audience. The first question from the audience that I will pose to any and all of the panelists who would like to respond comes from Lisette. She writes, "My brilliant disabled friend Naomi Ortiz shares a story in her book called *Sustaining Spirit* about how a friend taught her the difference between healing and mending, where mending is not a return to your previous state, but rather a transformation of yourself, where the wound may or may not be there anymore, but you are no longer who you once were. Is there a place for mending on the path to flourishing?"

Ann Millett-Gallant:

In my experience, I still have a lot of wounds visible, and because of what I went through following my accident, I can't use prosthetic legs anymore. I had too many problems with my knees and muscle contractions, this and that. And I thought, "It would just be more comfortable for me and less painful to just not use them at all." And once I did that, at first, I felt like I was losing something, but then I just became more comfortable doing things without them. So I mended in that way—I reoriented my perspectives and how I did things, and I stopped getting uncomfortable being on the floor around people. So that was a way of mending for me.

Karen Nakamura:

In terms of psychiatric disabilities, I don't know what healing and mending are. All of the cures we've been offered tamp down the symptoms, or at least some of the symptoms, but they don't really heal. They don't really cure. They don't really mend. Once you stop taking them, you're back to where you were, which is an odd trip. There's one term that has been used by some psychiatric activists in Japan, which I like, which is the word "recovery," from the language of Alcoholics Anonymous (AA). I don't like that it's from AA, but this notion of, "I am always a psychiatric disabled person, even when I'm doing well, even when I'm taking medications. It is always who I am. It's in my nature"—it's sort of like accepting who you are and working from there. I like that language, that I'm always in recovery. The dimensions that I don't like are that it takes away some of the activist component and puts the onus on myself.

Anand Prahlad:

It would be similar with autism. There's no mending or healing. I don't know that there's any mending or healing necessary because I don't think it's an illness. When I think of PTSD, or PTSS—trauma related to race—I think you have a trauma, and then there is the "after trauma." And in the period or the space of the after trauma, you can actually engage ideas like recovery or healing. But if you have trauma today, and then you have trauma tomorrow, and then you have trauma the next day, and that's your life, then where is the space for actual mending or healing? I think that's one of the really disturbing things about racial trauma: people aren't granted a post-traumatic space. So I don't think in terms of, as far as my own disabilities, healing in that way. I think of healing in moments, such as creative moments where one can transcend the trauma, or one can even make it into something else so that it's not what it was at the moment that you experienced it. If you practice yoga or you practice meditation, then maybe you're able at moments to take some of the trauma that's settled in your body out. But I don't know that that would be mending.

Joel Michael Reynolds:

I have a second question from the audience, and I'm not sure this person actually meant to have it thematically come together with the last one, but I think this will actually allow us to build on the comments you each just made. This question comes from Patricia. She writes, "I have mixed feelings about Rosemarie's discussion around 'broken' and 'fixed.' When one is recovering from a medical trauma with newly acquired disabilities, there is very definitely a feeling of being broken, when one is in a time of crisis and imbalance, et cetera. But as one adjusts and learns how to live with your new body, mind, the new normal, then, of course, that sense of being broken can shift to simply being okay, or maybe even greater." The point of this, from the person who wrote this question, I think is to say, Aren't there contexts in which it is and should be permissible and acceptable to consider oneself broken?

And I just want to add one little thing here. I think one of the reasons this conversation between the three of you is so rich and I felt like I've learned so much is that there has been a very strong interplay between psychological, psychiatric, and intellectual disabilities; physical disabilities; and disabilities that are quite clearly a result of societal injustices, inequities, and societal problems. The complexity of moving between each of these three domains and showing the ways in which they're connected and not cleanly separate has been coming out over and over again in our conversation so far. So maybe this question is an opportunity to circle back to the way in which there might be situations where, for example, feeling broken is okay. And Liz Bowen pointed out to me that, Ann, one of your paintings is actually called *My Beautiful Broken Brain*.

Ann Millett-Gallant:

Yes, I think what Rosemarie was saying, if you don't mind, is that people *think* in terms of it being broken, not that the person *themself* is broken. Instead, other people conceptualize that. And looking at the individual experience, I think that also should be open to interpretation. You know, I might consider myself broken one day about something that I'm upset about that day. I might feel broken from some of my experiences, but then I just find other ways to do things and try to deal with the pain—I use artwork. One reason why I say artwork is because it is a creative expression. And there's so many different interpretations to it, there's always more interpretations. And that's interesting to me, to study creative acts that can be both in terms of one's society and one's nationality and individual at the same time. Maybe it is the problem of classifying broken versus whole as absolutes. Broken means different things to different people at different times. That's something you have to overcome to mend completely.

Karen Nakamura:

There's a Japanese art form of repairing pottery with gold called *kintsugi*, where you use gold to repair, and you get some really beautiful pieces that have been repaired with that. In some ways, the broken and repaired piece is more beautiful than the original one. It reminds us, to go back to Prahlad's point, about the frailty and fragility of the world, that nothing will last forever, and that each break is unique, and each broken piece is unique. And how it comes back together is also unique. I don't think it's bad to refer to ourselves as broken at times. You know, certainly there are periods where my brain comes crashing down on me, and today is one of them. But these are the moments in which I am reminded of my humanity, reminded of my frailty, but they are also the moments that give me the energy to do things later on. So it's not always a negative to be broken.

Rosemarie Garland-Thomson:

Thank you for that comment. I want to suggest that I would want for us all to think that these conversations are less about what's permissible and not permissible, what's okay and not okay, but rather that what we're doing is exploring together and offering a variety of different perspectives, not rules, about how to think and be in the world as people considered disabled and people considered not disabled. One of the things I appreciate about the concept of the humanities is that it invokes the idea of the human, and the human is a way to yoke many of these differences and variations that human beings and the larger nonhuman world bring forward to us and to think about them. So I would not want my language and thoughts to be considered permissible or not permissible. Nonetheless, thank you for the comment about broken and unbroken.

Anand Prahlad:

When I think of "broken," I actually think of the medical creed: do no harm. But in fact, it's very difficult for medical professionals to treat people very often and do no harm. So sometimes the harm does end up leaving people feeling broken in ways that they weren't before they received those treatments. I don't think it's just necessarily whatever disabilities we might have before engaging with medical professionals. I think sometimes it's also the results, the side effects, of medical treatments that cause conditions that we might feel broken in this way or that way. And it's often a trade-off. If you have the feeling of brokenness and this other thing over here is managed better, is that a better situation than if you didn't have the brokenness and the thing over here was not being managed? So it can get complicated in that way.

Joel Michael Reynolds:

To make a personal comment, much of my psychiatric disability is a result of questions of grief and loss. Separating out what is in relationship to very specific events versus what is just a question of difference and of how I am—it's a question of difference and how I am that I sometimes feel very viscerally as being broken, and I sometimes feel very viscerally a sense of loss. That is a very complicated interplay, and one has to think about both environmental and structural factors and individual ones to even broach those types of issues.

There is another question from the audience that I want to make sure we get to, and I think this will take this last part of the discussion and open it up even further to one of our primary themes, not only today but in this series as a whole, that of flourishing. This comes from Greg, and he writes, "I understand Professor Prahlad to be reinterpreting flourishing so as to be lamenting limitations imposed by social factors, and at the same time, accepting personal limits as a feature of all human rights and embracing interdependence with others, including the natural world. I find this very attractive. Does it not, though, also raise a conceptual challenge for knowing how to ensure that human flourishing is a right enjoyed by all people? How can we know if one is close enough to being who one wants to be or having what one wants or feeling like one can be oneself to be described as flourishing?"

Let me try and rephrase this. As we balance the tension between accepting personal limitations and acknowledging the massive social limitations that are imposed on us, does acknowledging that tension raise a problem of knowing how we can tell whether or not someone is flourishing, and how we can establish a world in which there are human rights such that flourishing is maximized for as many people as possible? How do we translate these insights from today into questions of human rights? How do we make societies such that more people can flourish with the bodies and minds they already have?

Anand Prahlad:

I think maybe I would rephrase that as, Where do we begin, and how can we begin? Because to ask how we can accomplish it, I don't think we have enough time left to actually map that out. I think one of the main places we could begin is with a different kind of education in K–12 so that people graduate from high school with a different kind of sensibility about what it means to be a human being—what it means to be a human being relative to other lifeforms on the planet, and what it means to be a human being in this particular moment in which we're living in right now. And I say that with full understanding of how difficult it would be to transform educational institutions like the public schools. But a lot of things are difficult. I think it's a necessary thing that would make a big difference in the future trajectory of our society.

Karen Nakamura:

I think it's coming at universities across the nation. I have found that there is no university that hasn't had a rapid increase in the number of students who have nonapparent disabilities, whether it's psychiatric or developmental or neurological. And that, I think, is the success of the ADA. They have managed to thrive in kindergarten, elementary, middle-school, and college environments and had IEPs [Individualized Education Plans] that allowed them to come. Now they're coming to college, and they're finding barriers, and faculty are having to change. But in four or ten years, that wave is also going to come into society, and we can try to stop it and institutionalize them, but I don't think we can ever go back to that period. I think instead, companies and other places are going to have to figure out what to do with this generation of kids who have thought that the least restrictive environment is natural. That of course they have the right to thrive. Of course they have the right to be here. Of course they have the right to everything. So I have a lot of hope for the generation of kids who are born after 1990.

Joel Michael Reynolds:

Karen and Prahlad, you both brought up the question of younger people and especially people going through education, bringing us to another question from the audience. Michelle, from our public audience, asked, "What are people's views about parents making decisions about getting a cure for their young children? How do we help parents to consider all of these rich points that have been brought up about identity, pride, and difference with respect to their children?"

Karen Nakamura:

Talk to the adults who are living with that disability. Whether I think of the cochlear implants, whether I think of applied behavioral therapy, talk to the adults. So many times, it's just able-bodied neurotypicals who are making those decisions or advising. If you talk to Deaf people now about cochlear implants, they'll say, "Yeah, maybe have it for your child, but realize it's just a strong hearing aid. It won't make your child hearing. And so you should also accompany it with sign language and see which one your child wants. But they have the right to language exposure. So give them both, give them English and give them hearing." If you talk to adult autistics who have undergone ABA [applied behavior analysis] therapy, they'll say, "That was horrible. I spent all day with a therapist who was just teaching me how not to stim, and that's all we did. And that was such a colossal waste of time. There are so many more things I could have done with my life." But we never talk to the adults. And I think the thing is, you're not alone. There are other people who have gone through it, and they can share their experiences.

Anand Prahlad:

I would agree—that would be an important way that parents could become better educated about disabilities. On a macro-level, I think again, having some fundamental transformation of our social system would help. A lot of parents are really making decisions based on the fact that they can't take time off from work, or they are afraid that their children are going to be bullied, or they are afraid that their children are going to be left behind or have experiences in their school or in other situations where they are traumatized because of their difference. So I think if parents didn't have to be concerned with those kinds of issues, they would be a lot more open-minded about not necessarily looking for a "cure" for their children. I think a lot of it is just practical. If you're a single mother, for example, and you have three children, and you have to work two jobs in order to make ends meet, and you have a disabled child who requires a lot of attention, and then you're given the option for them to be "cured" or to receive some sort of treatment that would mean that their disability is not as noticeable or that it's momentarily fixed, you can understand there would be an inclination on the part of the parent to take that option. I think that part of it is really social circumstances that weigh on parents a lot of the time, that influence their decisions.

Joel Michael Reynolds:

I think that one of the really powerful things that came out in differing ways from each of your talks was the emphasis on how a society so fundamentally shapes what we take to be our individual choices, and those choices are often not really choices at all if you live in a society that's set up in a fundamentally unjust and inequitable manner, a society that doesn't offer universal pre-K, that doesn't offer parental leave, that doesn't provide sufficient supports for parents who have children with different needs, that doesn't offer universal healthcare. I might be referring to the United States in particular as an especially egregious example of a country presumably committed to life, liberty, and the pursuit of happiness and yet not actually providing the supports for that to become a reality for the vast majority of its citizens. Hopefully, someday that will change.

Speaking of politics, and we do not need to get into details here, but I think that this might be a really important thing to bring up. There has been a debate at the national level over the last few weeks about the meaning of infrastructure, and people have been noticing that in the infrastructure bill being discussed today, there are things like care for children, care for older people, et cetera. And my whole life, I've always been confused why infrastructure would only refer to roads and bridges when, if you don't provide infrastructure for caring for actual humans, what are we talking about? Nonetheless, combining a couple of questions from the audience, can you talk a little bit more about structural supports and infrastructure, and the relationship between questions of cure and supports that must be in place for us to even imagine a cure in a nonableist manner?

Ann Millett-Gallant:

Cure often suggests that someone doesn't need services that cost money anymore. That they don't need treatments of whatever kind that cost money—and that's problematic. And then things such as therapy in whatever form that a person needs to be funded, ultimately... I'm not an economist, so don't ask me where the money comes from. But, as you said, we need infrastructure for the humans too.

Joel Michael Reynolds:

We are nearing the end of our time, but I'd like to invite Rosemarie, Erik, and Liz if they feel like jumping in, and see if there are any further questions that they would like to ask, any comments, or any anything that's been said before that maybe you'd like to highlight and circle back to. Our speakers are amazing, and we get the great joy of working with them, but we've all had the blessing of being in email communication for about eight months now. So it's been a very collaborative process, and I know Rosemarie, Liz, and Erik might want to jump in here.

Rosemarie Garland-Thomson:

I'd be happy to begin by saying once again, thank you for these three presentations; to the National Endowment for the Humanities for funding this, to the Hastings Center for structuring this, to Erik and the other people at The Hastings Center; and also, for an opportunity to think about this incredibly challenging transformation that we have all gone through over the last year.

We've experienced many transformations, but I just want to call attention to one of them that Karen brought forward, and that is the transformation from what we think of as in-person work and in-person events and in-person life together in public and what we think of as virtual. That's one really crucial shift that's taken place in particular for people with disabilities because we—meaning people with disabilities—tend to use technology perhaps differently than nondisabled people, and I don't want to oversimplify this. As Karen has pointed out, as well as many of us who work in disability culture and disability studies, the world is designed for a particular kind of person and thus, technologies and the world we live in have not been built for, let's just say, the kinds of people who are involved as speakers and participants in these conversations.

It's so important to be able to think about how these transformational technologies are operating, how they are both our paths to access for people with disabilities and, at the same time, barriers to access and participation for people with disabilities. I want us to remember that part of what we're doing here in this series is to think about that.

This series began as an in-person event in New York. The first event was in-person in New York, and we thought to just videotape it and we'd make that available, buried somewhere on the website. We needed to transition to fully virtual events, and we've had now three more events. And they have evolved in terms of people's comfort level in using these, and in exploring these new complexities of disability and technology.

So I thank everyone for being able to address that in a complex way here and now. I think the record of these conversations will be really important in our retrospective glance at what this year has been like for people with disabilities. So thanks to all of us today for this and for the ongoing conversations.

Liz Bowen:

Rosemarie really summed it up here. I would just say thank you to all of you for the complexity and patience and flexibility that you've brought to this project and this process. One of the things that we've learned through organizing this series is how technology is often positioned as a kind of cure in itself, and even in conversations about disability, the idea that Zoom has made everything more accessible all of a sudden. And you know, we have learned while grappling with this platform that it can often be really difficult. Suddenly the interpreter is not visible, or suddenly the captioning is not working. For some people, the chat is really useful, and for some people, it's totally distracting.

There are all of these complexities that have to be navigated and I think one of the things that's really amazing about the disabled community is that we're all invested in working through that together and finding solutions and hacks, to use Karen's terminology. But what has been really powerful about working with you all and in the series is questioning the idea that there are these technological cures, either for our bodies or for the societal problems that we're grappling with.

Erik Parens:

I would only reiterate the thanks that Rosemarie and Liz have already offered. First of all, I cannot overstate how grateful I am for an opportunity to have a public conversation about the most complicated and important of questions. As Rosemarie said, we're not about legislating answers, we're about exploring questions, and there are few places left where people get to honestly explore together hard questions that don't have crisp answers.

We've been able to do that today because of these remarkable, wonderful speakers. Prahlad, Ann, and Karen, I am so grateful. I know everybody in the audience is so grateful to you for what you have given us today.

Liz Bowen:

Thank you to the National Endowment for the Humanities Deputy Director Patricia Brooks. From the Hastings Center, Mark Cardwell, Julie Chibbaro, Susan Gilbert and Danielle Pacia. Thanks to our sign language interpreters, Mary Darragh MacLean, Mike Barrios, and Jamie Hays, as well as our CART [communication access realtime translation] services from Karen Johnson, Andrew Hansen, and Amy Lee. And thank you to all of you in the audience who came here today and asked truly wonderful questions.

5

Enjoying

Disability as a Creative Force

Julia Watts Belser, Georgina Kleege, and Jerron Herman

Liz Bowen:

Hello everyone, and welcome to "Enjoying: Disability as a Creative Force." My name is Liz Bowen, and I'm the Rice Family Fellow in Bioethics and the Humanities at The Hastings Center. I am the associate director of *The Art of Flourishing: Conversations on Disability* series, along with my co-organizers Erik Parens, Joel Michael Reynolds, and Rosemarie Garland-Thomson.

With that, I will turn it over to my colleague Erik Parens, senior research scholar at The Hastings Center and Director of the National Endowment for the Humanities-funded Initiative on Bioethics and the Humanities.

Erik Parens:

Thanks to all of you for joining this conversation in our series, *The Art of Flourishing: Conversations on Disability*. The purpose of this Hastings Center series is to broadcast and to explore one fundamental theme, which is that people can flourish in all sorts of bodyminds. To flourish here means to exercise the capacities we have in pursuit of the goals that we find meaningful. We don't need different bodyminds to flourish; we need more supportive environments.

In her memoir *Too Late to Die Young*, the disability activist Harriet McBride Johnson describes the debate she had in 2002 with the bioethicist Peter Singer. As Johnson tells it, Singer pressed her to admit the necessary connection between disability and the absence of enjoyment. Full of confidence in the obviousness of his point, Singer challenged Johnson to imagine a disabled child on the beach watching other children play. Singer's challenge, of course, assumes that the disabled child on the beach cannot play. To Singer, it was self-evident that disability meant suffering; he could not imagine a disabled child finding pleasure in playing on a beach with their friends. And he certainly could not imagine that, as Harriet McBride Johnson put it, "there are pleasures that are peculiarly our own that are so bound up with our disabilities that we would not experience them, or would not experience them the same way, without our disabilities."

So, Johnson asserts, the task is clear. People with disabilities "need to confront the life-killing stereotype that says we're all about suffering. We need," she says, "to bear witness to our pleasures." And that's what we're here to do today, beginning with the remarks of our three wonderful activist-scholars.

Our first speaker today, Julia Watts Belser, is a scholar, rabbi, activist, and spiritual teacher whose academic home is Georgetown University. Julia's comments today are in the form of a prose poem with an interlude that includes an audio work she created with the disabled artist Claire Cunningham. In her comments, Julia will reflect on the joy of hiking in the woods in her wheelchair. She will reflect on the fact of her interdependence with other human beings and the natural world that makes such hiking possible. And, resisting simplification, Julia will invite us to consider the potential risks inherent in talking about enjoying disability.

Julia Watts Belser:

Thank you so much, Erik, for the wonderful invitation, and thank you all for this invitation to be in conversation with an amazing group of disabled scholars and artists, and with this extraordinary community of people who have gathered from all around the world.

I'm Julia Watts Belser. I'm a white Jewish woman with curly brown hair wearing a shimmery gray-pink shirt and a crocheted handmade kippah, a beret.

I want to begin with the title that we've chosen for today's event. I want to say a few words about the choice to center joy. I spend a lot of my time focused on disability and violence. As a scholar of religion and as a rabbi, it's my work to trace and try to transform the way religious texts and traditions have often done harm to people with disabilities, to women, to people of color, to trans and queer folk, to so many of us whose bodies and minds have been marked as other, as different, or as less.

At Georgetown, I direct a project on disability ethics and climate change, a project that has me examining how ableism, coupled with racism and white supremacy; economic inequality; gender violence; queer, trans, and fat hatred; and other forms of social and structural inequality make it more likely for people with disabilities to bear the brunt of climate disruption. It's hard, heavy, and urgent work. And I believe that fact makes it all the more crucial to talk and think about joy. I believe that joy is an essential part of the struggle, that it matters for us and for the world. I believe there is something radical and revolutionary about saying "yes" to pleasure, to satisfaction, and to savoring.

One of my beloved teachers, Ibrahim Farajajé, of blessed memory, used to say, "In the midst of it all, dare to bless the love."

This summer, I worked with disabled artist Claire Cunningham, a dear friend and longtime collaborator, a brilliant disabled dancer, choreographer, and performance-maker based in Glasgow, Scotland. We were commissioned to make a series of audio works called *We Run Like Rivers* for a public festival in Germany, examining disability in relation to ecology and wilderness and climate change.[1] For a couple of years now, Claire and I have been taking what we like to call "micro" hikes. Claire uses crutches, and I am a wheelchair user, so we don't exactly match the image most people have when they think of hikers.

One of the things we find, in fact, as we do this work, is that disabled folks are often imagined to not belong outdoors—like we are not supposed to go off the paved path or past the carefully curated spaces. But we are both drawn to wild places. I have an all-terrain hiking wheelchair that makes it possible for me to get into the woods. Claire describes herself as a four-footed creature, one who loves to explore rocky places, to probe those nooks and crannies. I'd like to share a three-minute selection from *We Run Like Rivers* that's built around those experiences in wilderness. It's a piece where Claire and I examine how lived disability experience shapes our relationship with land and our sense of connection with wild places.

[Audio clip begins with slow-building, soothing music.]

NARRATOR 1 (JULIA WATTS BELSER): Water runs over everything. And that feels like the motion of the wheel. Wheels are always in contact with ground in the same way that the river water is in seamless contact with the riverbed, the rocks. There's no break. When a walking person steps, there's a moment where they lift up from the ground, there's a disconnection. On wheels, there is no disconnection. That's something that feels really akin to the way a river runs.

NARRATOR 2 (CLAIRE CUNNINGHAM): I love being on rocks at the beach, really uneven land. I love those surfaces because they're like a puzzle that I need to work out how to traverse. The joy of sort of taking time with that. There's something else about being led by what the land allows you to do.

[The music grows a bit louder, featuring a quickly pulsating, yet nevertheless calming and melodic electronic beat.]

NARRATOR 1: The gentle downhill grade when the rolling is so easy.

NARRATOR 2: I really love turning into this sort of four-legged creature. All the little places that you can wedge the crutch really right into a corner or into a crack. In Scotland, we'd say nooks and crannies.

NARRATOR 1: It's the feeling of my whole body connected with, and intertwined with, the chair, who is also connected with, and intertwined with, the path. And that seamless, beautiful, easeful, effortless movement is what I associate with flow.

NARRATOR 2: And I get so lost in that sort of play with the ground; that becomes the only thing that exists in those moments.

[Music fades out.]

Julia Watts Belser:

One of the things that I love about this project is that Claire and I approach disability as a kind of knowledge. Rather than frame disability as a deficit, we ask, what does disability offer? What does it make possible? As a disabled artist, Claire pays particular attention to what she calls "disability expertise." What do we know as disabled folks? What skills do we have as disabled people? Not in spite of disability, but *because of* it, because of the difference of our bodies and minds, because of the particular ways we navigate the world.

Let me give you one example. As a manual wheelchair user, I am intimately connected with the literal lay of the land. I know the contours of every place I've ever lived on wheels: minute gradations in terrain, the flow of slope and surface, where the ground swells and how it rises, where the pavement cracks, the loose three bricks that play like a xylophone just outside the threshold of my office. That's the sound and feel of coming home.

In part *because* I am disabled, I pay attention to place. I don't mean some gauzy romantic notion of the land, but the actual tangible physicality of hill, grade, and gravity. I am always assessing. I'm always tracking my own physical capacity in relation to terrain. And because I pay attention—because I *must* pay attention—I notice qualities that others miss. Some years ago, a disabled friend who spent a lot of time in the hospital told me about the way the morning sun shined through their IV tubes, how the thin cannulas would catch the light and glow. And I thought, "Yes. Yes, this is something that I also know: how to turn toward what is, how to notice beauty, how to pay attention."

When I hike on wheels, I pay attention to the ground before me, partly because I have to, because if I get caught up in the vista and that view in the distance, I'll jam a caster wheel against a rock. But the practical demands have also built in me a capacity for recognizing that the land deserves attention—that it deserves my regard. The ground is my hiking partner, my companion in the journey.

I read terrain the way other folks might nod along with a companion's conversation. It's not exactly an equal partnership, though. The land can stop me in my tracks: a crevice, bulging tree roots, a wash out, a sudden drop. There's a moment in our audio piece that I just shared where Claire talks about being led by what the land allows you to do. I love that line, because it makes a powerful contrast with the conventional trope of overcoming limits or overcoming disability.

Part of the joy of the moment for me is figuring out what's possible right here, right now, in this place as I am. And part of the truth of it means coming face to face with limits. To hike, I need a certain kind of trail and a certain kind of weather. If it's rained a day or two before, the ground turns soggy and impassable. If my shoulders flare up, it can be weeks before I'm able to get back to the woods. Pain stops me sometimes. So do logistics. I can't go out without a hiking buddy and a driver, someone who can lift my wheelchair in and out of the car, someone who can help me pop my wheel out of a rut if I get stuck. I won't lie, that's often really frustrating.

In disability circles, it's common to hear folks lift up the value of interdependence, a challenge to the conventional American notion that independence is where it's at. Interdependence recognizes the way we depend on each other. It's built through mutuality, relationship care, and connection. Ecologists recognize interdependence as a fundamental truth of a well-working ecosystem. Life itself depends on the interconnected actions of often unseen or unacknowledged creatures—the insects and pollinators, the microbes that catalyze and decompose our flesh, the mosses, the fungi, the ants, the earthworms. So often we humans imagine ourselves above and apart, but we are creatures of an interconnected world. We need each other. We rely on each other.

But here's the other truth, the trickier truth, for me: Disabled folks don't get to ignore interdependence when it suits us. We don't get to shrug it off when it's inconvenient. And if I'm being honest, there are moments when I wish I could indulge in the illusion of an independent eye, that I could be spontaneous, go out without elaborate plans and counter plans without calling ahead to check the access routes, without assembling my own support team.

At the same time, as a white, well-resourced wheelchair user, I also know how deeply my own race, class, and access privilege shapes my ability to do what I love, to find and follow disability joy. There are risks when we talk about joy. We make joy a prescription or a requirement, a precondition for belonging. There's a risk that joy becomes just another way of judging: "Oh, if you're not happy, you're doing it wrong."

There's a risk that we look only to the inner dispositions and celebrate some people's capacity for finding satisfaction without attending to the material structural conditions that can make joy more likely for some of us, that can make pleasure more possible. Good health insurance, access to an income, material support for my own self-determination are just a few of the facts that buttress my own story. These are things that so many disabled folks are denied. That brings me back to the politics of joy, to the commitment I believe we must make to strive not just for a bare minimum of access but to build a world where all of us get access to pleasure, to satisfaction, and to joy.

Thank you.

Erik Parens:

Thank you, Julia, for those beautiful and deep reflections. Our next speaker is Georgina Kleege, who teaches in the English department at the University of California, Berkeley. Georgina is what she calls a "haptic docent," someone who uses the sense of touch to help others appreciate works of art. That is, she enables blind people to enjoy touch access to visual art, and she enables sighted people to get a sense of what it can be like to enjoy touch access. In her presentation, Georgina will describe how she and her collaborators have created choreographic and sonic art out of their encounters with a monumental sculpture by Richard Serra.

Georgina Kleege:

Hello. This is Georgina Kleege speaking. My name is Georgina Kleege, and I'm very happy to be here. And thank you, everybody, for attending, and thanks to Julia for leading us off. I'm going to describe an artistic interpretive collaboration I did a few years ago with an artist friend and collaborator named Fayen d'Evie. This was a project conducted at the San Francisco Museum of Modern Art (SFMOMA) under a program funded by the Mellon Foundation called the Artist Initiative. And the idea was that the museum invited contemporary artists to engage with pieces in their collection in different ways.

For the particular project that I was involved with, which was titled "Embodied Encounters," we were asked to collaborate with the conservation department at the museum and to work with pieces that had been on loan to the museum and were leaving, and then other pieces that were ephemeral or were being taken off of display due to conservation issues. And our project was meant to document these pieces present in the art museum in different ways.

Because Fayen d'Evie and I are both blind, our project focused on nonvisual perception and appreciation of art. Our co-collaborators were Bryan Phillips, who is a sound artist, and Shelley Lasica, who is a choreographer. As Erik introduced me, I identify myself in this project as a haptic docent. I came up with this term for myself because, as a blind person, I have enjoyed the incredible privilege of touch access to works of art in museums around the world, and whenever I'm offered an opportunity to touch art, I leap at the chance. And because I have all this experience, I've developed theories and practices around touch, tactile, and haptic experience of art. I have endeavored in various programs, particularly in museums in the Bay Area, to communicate those experiences to others who do not enjoy the same privilege, namely, sighted people.

The specific piece I'm going to be talking about today, as Erik introduced it, is a sculpture by the artist Richard Serra called *Sequence*, which was completed in 2006. The piece has found a home in various locations. When we were working on it in 2017, it was indoors at the San Francisco Museum of Modern Art, but it had been at the museum at Stanford University prior to that, and then in 2019 it returned to Stanford.

The piece is a monumental sculpture, very large. It's sixty-seven feet long, forty-two feet wide, and thirteen feet tall. It is made of waterproof steel, the type of steel with which ships are built. Those sheets of metal are about two inches thick. And the artist formed them into two nested *S* curves. An aerial view indicates that the form of the sculpture creates a kind of figure-eight or infinity shape. But when you're in situ, when you're in the site with the sculpture, since it's so tall, you can't actually see this. But the artist's idea is that the visitor actually enters the sculpture and moves through the sculpture in this figure-eight pattern. And then at various points during the path, you emerge into a kind of circular chamber inside the sculpture.

So, it is a choreographic object. It compels a certain kind of movement on the part of the viewer or visitor. Many sighted viewers find the experience somewhat disorienting because, as you're moving through the figure eight, you can't see very far ahead of you. You don't know what's coming. For myself, for blind people who are accustomed to navigating spaces without necessarily knowing what's happening in front of us, we felt that we wanted to explore this sculpture for potential as a choreographic object, to use our skills at blind navigation to document and to innovate different modes of moving through that space.

We also were interested in exploring the sculpture's potential as a sonic object. This idea came to me when I was sitting in the gallery at SFMOMA. There is sort of gallery seating there, a stadium-style seating there. I was sitting waiting for others to arrive or for something to happen. And, meanwhile, there were two kids in the sculpture running around at high speed, and periodically they would pause and one of them would shout, "Whoop!" And then the other one somewhere else in the sculpture would respond. And they kept this up for quite a while. The reverberation of their voices off the metal was quite satisfying, which was exactly why they were doing it, and it suggested to us different ways to explore the sonic potential of the sculpture.

This slide shows three of us inside one of the two central chambers of the sculpture (Figure 5.1). I am to the right. I'm a tall white woman with white hair dressed in black. I have my white cane at rest against my shoulder. Fayen is sort of in the middle of the image. She's also a white woman, and she has dark hair. She's holding a microphone pointed generally in my direction. And then Bryan Phillips, the sound artist, is crouched on the floor on the left with some sound equipment, and he has a whistle in his mouth, and his cheeks are puffed up to blow the whistle. Some of our blind

Figure 5.1 Georgina Kleege, Fayen d'Evie, and Bryan Phillips inside *Sequence*. Photo by Hillary Goidell.

navigation through the space involves different ways of producing sound and receiving sound. We whistled, we sang, we chanted, we clapped as the way to navigate, to signal to each other as we were moving through space.

We weren't allowed to touch the sculpture because we were in the museum and working with conservators. I have to note the irony of this. When the sculpture was on display, and is now once again, in an exterior space, all sorts of touching goes on, much more rigorous than simply touching with the fingertips. When the sculpture was moved into SFMOMA, the conservators discovered all sorts of dusty footprints up and down the walls of the interior. Apparently, there's a technique known to rock climbers where one can brace one's back against one wall and then walk one's feet up the other wall. So, this is something that people do to the sculpture. Nevertheless, we were abiding by the rules and avoiding touching the surfaces while we were working in the space. But we did obtain permission for me to do what is known as "shorelining" within the

ENJOYING 151

sculpture. Shorelining is a technique where a blind person using a white cane taps the tip against a wall, or sometimes a curb if you're an outdoor space, as a way to keep moving in a straight line or to follow the line—in this case of a curvilinear space. So, this was a form of navigation, but we also thought that it was interesting to think about the sonic repercussions of this. We obtained permission to hang a contact microphone on the sculpture and record the reverberations of the sound of my cane through the metal sculpture.

This is an image showing me on the left and Bryan on the right (Figure 5.2). I have my cane lifted up, and I'm reaching toward a wad of tape at the end of the tip of the cane. In order to do this work, the conservators required us to come up with something to wrap around the tip of my cane so that the actual tip was not touching the sculpture. And we had to experiment with all sorts of things, different types of plastics and different types of tape. Here, Bryan and I are both smiling because this was quite a protracted testing experience. Eventually, we came up with something. The negotiation

Figure 5.2 Georgina Kleege and Bryan Phillips with a cane. Photo by Hillary Goidell.

was that we wanted something to wrap the tip to protect the sculpture, but we also didn't want to deaden the sound. It took a while to find something that was appropriate. The process had a side benefit to the museum, which was that every time that I went through the sculpture doing this process with my cane, it collected dust bunnies, so I would come out of the sculpture with great wads of dust on the end of my cane. So, I was performing a cleaning function.

All right, this is an image of myself on the left doing the shorelining, tapping my cane against the surface to sort of guide myself with the cane (Figure 5.3). Shelly Lasica, our choreographer, is on the floor semi-recumbent with her back to the camera and one arm slightly raised. She was composing a choreography in response to the form of the sculpture. Here she was responding to the curves of the walls. I don't know that it's apparent from the photograph, but the walls are not perpendicular to the floor. They're often curving inward overhead. So, she was performing some moves to simulate the feeling she got from the walls without actually touching them.

Figure 5.3 Georgina Kleege shorelines as Shelly Lasica composes choreography. Photo by Hillary Goidell.

ENJOYING 153

Figure 5.4 Georgina Kleege and Shelley Lasica outside *Sequence*. Photo by Hillary Goidell.

This is an image of myself and Shelly outside the sculpture (Figure 5.4). The sculpture here is visible as a diagonal line taking up almost half of the image on the right. We are walking around to map the circumference of the sculpture, its footprint. We are matching each other's stride. We are practicing a kind of choreography to map the form of the sculpture so that later when we went to Stanford to the empty plot where it had once stood, we could reproduce the choreography of the sculpture.

Incidentally, we did the same sort of learning of the layout inside the sculpture, walking and eventually running up the figure eight, walking and moving at different paces to learn the choreography of the sculpture. This process was, interestingly enough, hard to document in the photograph, mainly because the photographer couldn't get far enough ahead of us. So, there were a few images, for instance, of my cane peeking around the curve.

The next image shows when we moved our operations to the site at Stanford, at the plot of cement where the sculpture had lived, and

154 THE ART OF FLOURISHING

Figure 5.5 Bryan Phillips records the sound of Georgina Kleege's cane. Photo by Hillary Goidell.

since 2019 has now returned (Figure 5.5). I'm there with my cane in front of me. Bryan is to one side of me with a mic pointed toward the ground, attempting to pick up the sound of my cane. Our ability to perfectly replicate the choreography of the sculpture in the site was a little bit impaired because the museum had placed a couple of smaller sculptures by other artists in the space. So, we kept sort of bumping into things, but we were able to replicate some of the choreography of the sculpture.

This is an image of me again at Stanford. I'm reaching down with my hands and bending over to touch the ground so you see the top of my head (Figure 5.6). Since the sculpture weighs some 235 tons, it did leave a trace in the slab there outside the museum. You could feel various contact points that were left behind. The image documents a memory that I still retain, which feels a little sad; there is a certain degree of regret while feeling the trace of the sculpture but remembering a different experience of the sculpture. That is to say, I'm feeling the trace with my fingertips, but my experience of the sculpture was not about its tactility. It was more about

ENJOYING 155

Figure 5.6 Georgina Kleege touches the ground. Photo by Hillary Goidell.

kinesthesia and proprioception, movement, and the movement of the body through space.

To conclude, I'll say that when museums provide access to visual art for blind and visually impaired visitors, it's often done in a top-down manner where the cultural institution delivers information about the artwork to people considered to be outside of the experience. This intervention meant to flip that script and to bring our blindness into the museum, and to offer alternative methods of navigation, of tactility, of proprioception, of kinesthetics, and of aesthetics, to bring nonvisual forms of art appreciation into the space. Thank you.

Erik Parens:

Thank *you*, Georgina, for those generative reflections! Jerron Herman, our final presenter today, is a disabled dancer and writer on art and culture. Jerron will first show his film *Hearth/Kitchuns* and then reflect on the creative force that he explains is necessary to transform a kitchen into a hearth—[that is], the force that is necessary to transform a space of mere productivity into a space of pleasure. Indeed, be prepared to enjoy in Jerron's film the sheer enjoyment of three dancers as they, in a sunlit hearth, share glasses of wine, grapes, and each other's company.

Jerron Herman:

Hello. My name is Jerron Herman. I'm a dark-skinned Black man with bleached blond hair, and I'm wearing a blue button-up long-sleeved shirt. I'm equally delighted to be here discussing the interconnected realities of disabled joy in relation to creative force, how flourishing needs a series of other complex agreements that rest in and out of the bodymind, how we must budget for incongruity, how incongruity is not failure. As my other panelists have elucidated the products of a disability expertise and its crucial invisible contributions to support environments, I wish to offer a note on joy myself. My experience with this topic furthers because, as Erik said it, I'm a disabled dancer, and I experience a dizzying alternation between desired typical embodiment and a decidedly disabled body that acts without regard to organization or the repeated facilitation of movement. Repeatability is a critical function of productivity, a litmus for mechanized sanitation, a promise of efficiency.

What is the cost, then, of a glitch or a stall, a stutter, a misstep? My internal inquiry is largely not knowing exactly what I just did. This is beautiful to me, as it feels like a walk among intertwined rocks on the beach, as described by Claire Cunningham in her and Julia's *Flow // Crip Joy*, around the sinuous ruins of a multi-ton sculpture, exemplified in Georgina's presentation on museum access.

I must trouble the objective of my expression. In my art offering, I highlight the pleasurable inefficiency of use. It's too much, for it skirts necessity and is sometimes cacophonous. I'm actually more interested in a form of theatricality that subverts a clichéd identity with joy. Joy can operate in an elevated—too much—luscious way. And its use in the disabled body is intrinsically rapturous. Now, I would like to invite us to watch this film, *Hearth/Kitchuns*. And I also invite you all to modify the audio in your own way. As I said, it is cacophonous at times.

Audio Description from *Hearth/Kitchuns* (written by Joselia Hughes):

Sunlit and blurred by haze, Jerron stands, stretches, in an eating area and in front of a doorway. From a variety of angles, he pulls one arm down, hand cupped. Repeat or glitch or repeat. Same arm overhead: a diver's suggestion. Jerron swivels and shifts his body to the hint of a prayer. A child playing little teapot, a flower stem bracing for the puckered blow of pursed lips and full lungs. A diver plunges again. Hand traces neck; hand half circles head; caressing hair. Bird chirps beak break into instrumental song. Jerron greets Alice, a mixed woman who's in a wheelchair. They share a warm hug. Jerron twirls Alice. Laurel, a white woman who's in a manual wheelchair, enters. Jerron and Laurel embrace, Laurel's head cradled in Jerron's arm. Alice releases a boisterous laugh. All three smile through sunshine's joy. They bow, bodies becoming stems in bend from a gentle breeze. All rise to extend their arms in bloom, palms face-up, circle palms out, in offerings' service. They hold their palms face up, then dive their arms, fingers clenched together as the nose of a descending fish. They roll their backs, spin, pull, elongate. Repeated gestures. Laurel approaches camera and breaks fourth wall by holding up a glass of wine. All three toast at the table. Jerron eats a red grape. Music fades and Alice, without wheelchair, is on the floor. She straddles the doorframe and winds her body to flip in the narrows of the passageway. Music resumes. Belly down, Alice grabs her glass of wine, tucks her legs into child's position and extends her wine glass to the fourth wall. Laurel enters the kitchen and opens the freezer and quickly bows forward with her wine glass in hand. She curls up her body into drinking position. She drinks. She places her empty glass on the counter. Jerron behind the stove holds his glass and drinks. As he drinks he stoops slowly behind the stove. He pops up with a silly grin, holdings his glass above his head. Alice, on the floor, bends backwards to reach for her glass. Laurel turns in the kitchen, reflections of Alice and Jerron in the face of the microwave. Jerron behind the stove bends his body into a glider, arm stretched back, head held high. Cut back to gauzy footage of Jerron stretching arm down. Cut to all three toasting at the dining table. Glitch or repeat or glitch. Four places set, three places in use. Alice, Jerron, and Laurel joke together. Alice eats a grape, and the birds chirp in the dark. And the birds chirp in the dark. *Hearth/Kitchuns* by Jerron Herman, featuring Laurel Lawson, Alice Sheppard, AD: Joselia Hughes, Music: Ketsa (CC BY-NC-ND). Thanks to 3981.

Jerron Herman:

The diverse frequency of kitchen use to me supports a timeline that mirrors disabled embodiment within the home. Atypical processes are satisfied as much at 3 a.m. as they are at 6 p.m. The expressions of productivity and the stuff of ease have essentially thinned during this time anyway. The choreography of rolling out of bed to a call is no longer detested but understood. The relationship to homebound is now unpitied—heroic, even. The shock of perpetual inertia inspired a perpetual task, to architect found space, to build. Folks determine to delineate, refurbish, and imbue meaning in their homes to counter the perceived indignity of cold efficiency or the perceived indignity of mere pleasure.

This is a reality that most disabled people understand implicitly. The frequency through which we must adapt and architect found space to make it habitable, professionable, and pleasurable is constant. But there is a grade of that activity which demonstrates our creative force. This force seems to be precisely central to the transformation of the kitchen into a hearth, whether in a disabled imaginary or not. This transformation is necessary to uphold the difference between productivity and pleasure. Why else do we differentiate between cooking, preparing, and making dinner? The hearth means multiple perspectives and equally multiple pleasures. I think the hearth is altogether another realm, one that travels between stoic productivity and sensuous meaning. You have your kitchen: appliances, function, obligation, and society. You have your hearth: created, ritualized, inspired, desirous.

The hearth is actually an amalgam of the kitchen's purposes, one of which is alluded to with the Ebonics spelling of "kitchuns," K-I-T-C-H-U-N-S, to refer to the nappy locks of a Black child's hair. That reference is built around the practice of relieving naps in the kitchen or nearby, as slaves had no room delineations. And yet, naps were cared for next to food preparation and bathing. I use it in the title to mark some people's long understanding of multi-use. There is the shell, and then there is the spirit in everything, it seems. The fun is examining where the effluence appears.

Hearth/Kitchuns was developed for the opening session of the Disability Futures convening, hosted by the Ford Foundation, to express a corner of the disability arts movement. The film centers on a singular phrase that revolves around the body to elicit comfort, which is then made variable across different embodiments and scenes. Hosting the phrase in the hearth highlights the importance of abundance. Within the film, images settle to communicate that the kitchen is a social center, which was expressly heightened by our pandemic reality. The kitchen in the film is not mine, but a friend's, as I was in the middle of a residency in California. Featuring Kinetic Light's Alice Sheppard and Laurel Lawson, our kitchen was especially symbolic. Our intentional community was dotted by our warm hellos and clinks at a toast. The ensuing highlighted bits of kitchen focused on theatricalized pleasure: opening the refrigerator for a snack, enjoying the entryway, and scoping the oven island, all with coordinated choreography. It was satirical to heighten this normal space with elevated movement. The satirizing continued with a wink throughout Joselia Hughes's poetic audio description. Joselia wrote equally emblematic phrases that would describe a disabled body within a disabled film, broadening what images were important.

In editing, I chose to, at moments, obfuscate the descriptions behind the score and the soundscapes. We were at a dinner party preparing an oral practice that we honed in communal situations. I wanted to identify elements of pre-pandemic to relay the continued occupation in this new world. The sound design is itself entirely absurd. Disjunctive and caustic sometimes, but I feel a warmth about it, like the heater in my childhood home that produced this incessant whirring noise during cold snaps. It would hum to me at a decibel loud enough to hear, but far below annoyance. I associated warmth and security with that hum, and I would happily drift off. The soundscapes also are associated with our shared memory of birdsong or wheeled movement, or dinnerware. That warmth or inner life of the hearth is evident after I bid hello to Alice and Laurel. We all settle into a trio of the phrase I foregrounded. How did we know it independently? And how does it rest in our bodies after? It's interestingly cinematic, like an old musical that suddenly bursts into song. We need our ordinary spaces to be written larger, and this was one of the offerings that I think did that. Thank you so much.

Rosemarie Garland-Thomson:

Thank you very much, Julia, Jerron, and Georgina, for those really amazing presentations. It was a pleasure to join you and to think more about disability joy as well as disability creative expertise. I'm Rosemarie Garland-Thomson. I am a silver-haired senior woman with pale skin and red computer glasses, and I'm joining you here today from my home office in San Francisco. I'm very glad and honored to be here to conduct this gently facilitated conversation among the three panelists today.

We're going to spend ten minutes in this conversation, the purpose of which is to allow or facilitate the three of you to be able to engage with one another. And then we will move on to questions from the audience that the three of you can address together. So I'll begin with my main question, and we may have other questions along the way. For Julia, Georgina, and Jerron, can you tell us more about how the distinctive shape and movement and use of your bodies has contributed to the development of your art practice, to the new embodied art forms that you've developed? In other words, how has living in and with bodyminds considered disabled enabled you to make distinctive art forms? Julia, would you like to start?

Julia Watts Belser:

Sure. I'll be happy to start, thanks. Thank you so much for the question, Rosemarie. I love this question because it names something that often feels counterintuitive. Growing up as a disabled person, I was taught to minimize disability at every opportunity. Whether or not I was successful at it, the goal was to shrink down disability, to make disability and my own access needs take up as little space as possible. Whenever my disability complicated something, I was supposed to shrink down those complications, regardless of what it cost me.

Now, as a creative person and as a scholar, as somebody who thinks about disability and art and spirituality and religion, everything I do is built on flipping that script. The key question I ask now is, "Actually, can I pay more attention to disability? Can I really make more of this?" I don't mean make myself more disabled. I mean, "Can I pay more attention to what disability makes possible and to what it brings in the world?" Earlier, I gave a couple of examples of that when I was talking about the way that my own disability experience forces me to do certain things; at the same time, disability both allows and requires certain things of me. There's a sweet spot there between "allow" and "require," which makes possible a different kind of attention as I move through the world, both the natural world and the built environment. Thanks. I'll pass it on now to Jerron.

Jerron Herman:

Thank you, Julia. And I would say I totally commiserate with you in that—though, I guess, not necessarily with the compulsion, or the feeling of being compelled, to shrink my disability. I was actually afforded a liberal advantage by my parents to seek out my community, but I was too afraid to seek it out as an adolescent. And I, by my own measure, minimized my disability or my understanding of disability until I became a dancer. And it was in that that I do believe a true disability aesthetic that communicated a kind of liveliness to a disability embodiment was introduced to me. So, I attach art practice to disability all the time, and it's very intrinsic and important to me. The rigor of developing a piece is not unlike the rigor of understanding embodiment, nor is it unlike the scholarship and research and community that is purposeful and necessary to even build a good piece of work. And I find those parallels also with respect to faith and relationship to a kind of . . . understanding of, in a weird way, endowed being, this endowed space of embodiment. It feels like a responsibility, at the end of the day; and through that kind of lens, I do also think about disability as not just my own, but to be prompted, seasoned, and experienced with others.

Rosemarie Garland-Thomson:

This is Rosemarie again. Georgina, I imagine you want to comment as well, but I first wanted to insert a comment in our conversation in response to what Julia said and what Jerron is saying about the training that we get as people with disabilities growing up. I wanted to add the idea that the training I got growing up about being disabled and living with a body considered disabled was to deflect. So, for me, because I have very unusual arms, it was deflection that I learned, and that was, "Don't pay attention to my arms. Pay attention to my mouth." And that's how I then learned to really be a teacher, someone who could do something with their mouth, with words. And that was liberating for me as a person with a disability. So, thank you for that concept about shrinking and the opportunity to add the concept of deflecting from my own experience. Georgina, did you want to finish up and say something about your own experience in relation to this question?

Georgina Kleege:

All right. Thanks, Rosemarie. I sort of echo things that both Julia and Jerron, and you, have said about what sounds like similar experiences growing up and being trained. In my case, it was sort of an unspoken training, I think. It wasn't anything that anybody said to me. But it was implicit that it was more acceptable to somehow downplay or keep silent about the experience of disability. Going alongside that and maybe fighting against it, I think there still exists in the world the kind of myth of compensatory powers because people are very ignorant about disability and the disability experience. There's this sort of belief that, for instance, because blind people lack one sense, they have extra powerful hearing and touch, and so on and so forth. And in the work that I have been doing, I really wanted to get away from that and to say that it's not about having an extra sense. It's more about redirecting attention to the other senses and other modes of navigation, other modes of interacting with objects and spaces that one learns. And in recent years, I've really cultivated and developed techniques to do things that in some sense I had been doing since childhood. But now, you know, I've sort of named them and done them more deliberately.

Julia Watts Belser:

Related to what Georgina and Rosemarie said, I'd love to add that I really resonate with this idea of directing attention. I think one of the things that has been so interesting for me for my current practice has been directing attention specifically into my experience of impairment, not away from it. I want to call attention to a very dangerous dynamic that happens sometimes, a deflection strategy for navigating ableism in the world. For example, as a wheelchair user—a physically disabled person—one of the deflection strategies I learned was to say, "Oh, you know, I can't run, I'm not good at moving, but I'm very smart." This is a strategy we absolutely must resist because of the way it does tremendous harm to people with cognitive or intellectual disabilities. It reinforces the idea that a certain kind of intelligence is a prerequisite for being accepted and valued. I reject that. So I want to draw attention to the way that there are dangers here. I'm inviting myself and also all of us to reflect on that question of what happens when we refuse that logic and say no to those kinds of hierarchies as well. It's an important thing to think about, to name, and to resist.

Rosemarie Garland-Thomson:

I thank you and everyone else. We need to wrap up here, but I do want to emphasize what Julia said about how refusing disability

ENJOYING 165

categories in ourselves can also reinforce disability prejudice and discrimination in others. And I think that cautionary note is extremely important as we think about the resourcefulness and generativity that disability experience and lives lived with disability have given us. It's a reminder to, at the same time, be inclusive and humble—and I think we all have been humble—but it's a reminder of the infinite wonder and variety of disability experience and to honor that as fully as we possibly can. So, thank you very much.

Joel Michael Reynolds:

Hello, everyone. My name is Joel Michael Reynolds. I'm a white guy wearing a dark blue shirt that definitely makes the circles under my eyes look worse. I think this was a bad decision, but it's too late now. I'm having a good hair day, so I guess that balances it out. I'm also wearing glasses and have a number of piercings on the nose, ears, and the like; I have dark hair. I am very happy to be lightly moderating the public Q&A session. This has already been such a fantastic event, and I'm happy to see all of the wonderful, wonderful questions we've got from people. This first question is from an anonymous attendee: "One thing that strikes me is the role of aids or artifacts, for example, our canes, wheelchairs, and various other tools and material artifacts we use to interact with the world. Where do bodies begin and end, and where do artifacts begin and end? Do you see these as separate? Do you see the relationship as cocreated? Can you talk a bit about this relationship?"

Julia Watts Belser:

I'd be happy to speak to that. This is Julia. I'm really interested in the relationship between me as a disabled person and my wheelchair, and I'm particularly interested in the lush, messy interplay between us. I don't think of my wheelchair as an "it," as an object, yet I do recognize us as two distinct beings. I get really interested in thinking about the kind of creative synergy that comes from almost always being in relationship with my wheels. Part of the thing about wheels is they don't actually always do what I want. I mean, bodies are like that too! I think there's a kind of element of that interaction that feels really lively and important to pay attention to.

Georgina Kleege:

I will add to that. This is Georgina. I'm just thinking about my use of the white cane, what it means to me. Of course, it's a navigation tool for me. It extends touch from my hand to the ground and perhaps walls around me. It's also a sonic tool to some degree, in that you can tell something about the space, the surfaces that you're moving on, with the sounds that the cane makes. But the cane also—and I think most significantly—serves as a signifier of blindness. So, it's a sign to others that this person holding onto this white thing can't see. And that's going to alter the way I interact with others, particularly others who are driving vehicles. So, where the cane is most useful is, for instance, in walking around a city street and coming to an intersection with no stoplight but with a stop sign, and then the car pulls up to the crosswalk, and they want to wave you across. Well, that only works if that person can see, and so the white cane functions to say, you're going to have to come up with a different method of communication besides simply waving through your window.

Jerron Herman:

This is Jerron. I don't use any devices, and so the legibility of disability for me is continuously in flux. And I think that normative play is really interesting and challenging, and sometimes I wish I had a cane.

Joel Michael Reynolds:

Thank you for that. I want to combine two questions that I think get at a similar kind of concern, but in slightly different ways. The first one asks, "What was the most helpful resource you had in your journey of joy, self-acceptance, and self-identifying?" And I want to combine that question with another: "Any advice for a newly disabled twenty-seven-year-old who previously had been almost aggressively independent and is struggling to come to terms with her new self-image, particularly regarding mobility aids? My logical mind knows I have nothing to be ashamed of, but I still find my own issues stopping me from fully participating in life."

Georgina Kleege:

This is Georgina. I could address both those questions. I think for me—and so I would turn this into advice—the greatest resource has always been other disabled people. When I was a young person, I became blind at ten years old. It wasn't until I was perhaps twenty that I really had much contact with other blind people or other disabled people in general. And there was such an impetus to downplay my disability, to not appear to be different and try to not appear to be different, to not talk about it, not talk about the experience.

However, when I started to meet other blind people and people with other types of disabilities, it was incredibly liberating. And I think, initially, there was some hesitation, and I know this happens to a lot of people who are newly disabled: that fear of, "Oh, I'm not disabled enough, or people won't accept me as a part of the community because I'm a newcomer and so on and so forth." I've never found that to be the case. In fact, I actively, socially, professionally, and artistically gravitate toward other people with disabilities because I know that there's some shared experience. It's not the same, but there are commonalities. And that has always been supportive for me.

Jerron Herman:

This is Jerron. Our community is so diverse that I wouldn't even begin to try to set up an understanding around your own self-identification with, you know, a mere allegiance to our community. I would say go a bit deeper than just identity to support other aspects that can be communal. In my case, I think that the contributing factor to finding community was making it be rooted in dance, in something that I was also interested in. And even within that, you know, there are some people in my community that I disagree with, though I think that what connects us is our shared occupation and our shared vision for continuing or intervening for our industry or for our slice of life. And that has bred new conversations and deepened the ways that we do find connectivity. It's interesting to think about: Have I had a relationship that was not akin to work, you know, or akin to developing some aspect of art or community activity? Like, do I just have a disabled friend that has nothing to do with my work? I don't know.

Julia Watts Belser:

Disability arts were also—disabled dance in particular—transformative for me. When I saw AXIS Dance perform for the first time, I had been using a wheelchair for about a year. As a new wheelchair user, I was still in a period in my life where I felt quite ungainly on wheels and also just awkward in general, because I was afraid of occupying the space. Seeing AXIS Dance was a major transformation for me, because I realized, "Oh, you could go big, you could go bold! And it could be amazing." Of course, I couldn't dance like any of those dancers did—but I held on to that vision, that feeling.

I actually got to know disability a lot more through books, art, and other media before I started meeting a lot of disabled people in the flesh. So that's a resource worth considering, as well.

I'll add one other resource that's been important to me: a practice of self-tenderness. When I am experiencing grief or frustration or just feeling mean to myself, I've developed a practice of offering very deliberate tenderness to the joints and parts of my physical body that aren't able to do what they had done before. That's become really important to me. I summon up that tenderness and offer it to my knee and my hip, and that's allowed me to shift some of the experience. If that strategy is useful to anyone, please feel free to try it out for yourself.

Joel Michael Reynolds:

That dovetails very nicely with the next question. We actually got at least three different versions of this question. And I'll read just one of them: "With respect to the idea that disability doesn't automatically mean suffering, what about disabled people with chronic pain conditions and disabled people who do live in chronic pain, constant pain?" And they write, "You know, for me, this is suffering. I do have disabled pride; I love all of us disabled people. But what about those of us for whom, you know? Yeah."

Julia Watts Belser:

I'm happy to say something. I don't have chronic pain, so I can't speak specifically to that experience, since it isn't my own. But pain is a part of my own disability experience. The kind of inherited strategy that I had for dealing with pain was wait for it to be gone. Wait for it to be over, and then the good times can start again. My disability experience has been making me rethink that strategy. That strategy doesn't work for me, and I think what has been most interesting and most fruitful for me is to not try to push away pain. Instead, I've been trying to let pain be part of a complex story. There are moments, at least in my life, where pain and joy can live together, where pain and a sense of intricate attention to the present moment can live together. I mean, it doesn't always work for me, but at times it can be useful, this practice of holding pain together with other things, where I'm just trying to cultivate my own sense of gentleness with it.

For me, it's been helpful to make a distinction between pain and suffering. That is to say, sometimes I have pain, and I suffer a lot with it. Sometimes I have pain, and it's a part of the fabric of my experience. I find that I'm often suffering more when I'm invested in trying to deny pain, or push it away, when I hate it or go to war with it. That's been my own experience.

Joel Michael Reynolds:

It is possible, I think, to both take pride in something that is negative, in the ways it impacts oneself, and, at the same time, wish that negativity, or some of the negative aspects of it, to go away. And some of the, I think, most nuanced discussions I've read about in disability studies—and also just discussions I've been a part of as an activist in other community spaces—are about being open about that tension and, instead of positing that as a tension, admitting that lives are just really, really complex. And I have psychiatric disabilities. One of them is depression. And there is a way in which I definitely would rather not have a major depression. And there are things that I actively do to mitigate its effect on my life. And, at the same time, it's very clear to me how it shapes who I am; I would not be who I am right now without that shaping effect.

And I want both to be able to say that we should have certain treatments available for people with depression and to have a neurodiversity kind of approach that states that depression is a part of the way humans are. I want to have both of those things at the same time; and I don't think it's inconsistent or wrong to admit that sort of complexity we're talking about in life. Life is complex and messy, and I think that that's how things like this work.

There's also, I think, a very significant difference between forms of constant pain that are consuming and forms of constant pain that still allow a person to move through life. If you have a migraine to the point that you cannot get out of bed—you cannot open your eyes to see the light if you're sighted, and if you move, you immediately start vomiting—that's a very different sort of experience than other forms of constant pain, and also different than the negativity that might come along with certain other types of impairments. We need a rich set of ways of thinking about these things that admits these many differences.

Julia Watts Belser:

Joel, what you're saying is very wise. I think it's also really dangerous to try and make meaning out of pain. Sometimes individual people figure out a strategy or a framework for meaning-making that works well for them, which is great. But it's dangerous and risky to then suggest that as a strategy for others or as a meaning for everyone. When we're talking about pain, as you're saying, Joel, there are so many different types and experiences of pain in relation to disability. We need to recognize and acknowledge the differences in people's experience of pain, the way that pain can have a quite different character for different people, or at different moments in our lives. Because of that, I'm very suspicious—and would like us all to be suspicious—of the idea that we can tell a neat story about pain, or to deny it and suggest it isn't a part of disability experience.

Joel Michael Reynolds:

I'm going to do another double question, because these two fit together really well. The first is from an anonymous attendee who asks, "What are some things you'd like museums to do in order to provide a more experiential kind of inclusion?" And I want to pair this concrete question with one that's slightly more abstract from our own Liz Bowen, who writes, "Can you talk about the role of access in your work? A lot of people, perhaps the majority of people, think of checklists, or they think of accommodations when they think of access, and that everything has to be done in a certain way so that things are equitable. But Jerron's piece in particular complicates that idea, right? The moments where the audio description becomes harder to hear actually replicate the experience of a dinner party when it's loud and chaotic and you're missing things, which is its own kind of access. Right? But it's a very different kind of access than making sure every moment is clearly communicated and always the same way." And she concludes by saying, "How do you all think about the meaning of access in your work?" So, can you talk about the theoretical and the very kind of practical levels of that?

Georgina Kleege:

This is Georgina, maybe I'll take that up, specifically regarding the museum setting. Thinking against the idea of a compliance checklist, in a lot of my work I've been trying to communicate the idea that access goes both ways. That is to say that disabled people want access to the mainstream culture, but I think mainstream culture wants access to disabled people. Disabled people have something to contribute, whether that be new forms of knowledge, or new types of experience that haven't been much represented or included in the past.

Specifically, my work as a haptic docent has been trying to model this, to say, "Okay, you give me this incredible privilege that I can come into your museum and take a touch tour." And you know, every time I've done that around the world, people with me—but also other strangers who witness me doing this—they really want to know what it's like, you know, because everybody wants to get their hands on art, and everybody isn't allowed to do that. Therefore, I feel it's like a cultural obligation I must communicate what that experience is like and to open up that experience to other people. Yeah, maybe I'll stop there and hear from Jerron or Julia.

Jerron Herman:

Yes, this is Jerron. I absolutely love that in terms of the reciprocal nature of institutions and the disabled community as it pertains to the values, culture, and products that we offer to make it incredibly marketable. I would say there's something really important to me about access as a framework to counter hyperproductivity. In general, access is a way in which we test ourselves with understanding how to relate to folks who are right in front of us in order to narrow the impact of a global conversation to a local feeling. I think that access has this way of zeroing in on who's in the room in a way that is authentic and messy as well. It's informed by the people in the room; it's informed by the vision of the host. In really real ways, I think that the work of *Hearth/Kitchuns* is to extrapolate on, What are the aspects of hosting that access kind of produces? And it's to maybe theatricalize that as well, which I think is a process of inviting someone into your home and in what ways would you do that. And that, for me, is access. It's giving people enough information to make their own decisions and also understanding the aesthetic of the host.

Julia Watts Belser:

I love that. I was thinking that we often think too narrowly about access and what it can be. If checklists help get some basic access built into spaces, that's great. But they're only the very beginning of the story, like the absolute ground floor, not the completion of the work. Access is about questioning and rethinking norms. Whom do we expect to be in a space, and whom is a space built for and made for? To really do better at access, we have to go into the very frameworks of the norms, conventions, and expectations of not just physical spaces but also of the environments in which we live, work, and move. I want to see what happens when a group of intentionally, deliberately diverse disabled folks are at the forefront, when things are being designed and plans are being made. That gets us to a really different conversation about access than the kind of grudging add-on, supplemental, afterthought access that we often end up with.

Erik Parens:

What a beautiful and important event! Huge thanks to our wonderful speakers, Julia, Georgina, and Jerron, and to our wonderful moderators and facilitators, Rosemarie, Joel, and Liz.

6

We Belong to One Another

Disability and Family-Making

Jina Kim, Jess Waggoner, Sami Schalk, Joseph Stramondo, Leah Smith, and Mia Mingus

Liz Bowen:

Thank you all for joining us, and welcome to "We Belong to One Another: Disability and Family-Making." My name is Liz Bowen. I'm a postdoc at The Hastings Center and the associate director of this series, *The Art of Flourishing: Conversations on Disability*. I helped to organize this series along with my colleagues Erik Parens, Joel Michael Reynolds, and Rosemarie Garland-Thomson. To start us off with a quick visual description, I'm a millennial, a white woman with brown hair, and I'm wearing what I call my "academic uniform," a black mock neck shirt and a silver chain. There is a wall behind me and some various parts of my living room. With that, I will turn it over to my colleague Erik Parens, who is director for the National Endowment of the Humanities-funded Initiative in Bioethics and the Humanities at The Hastings Center.

Erik Parens:

Thank you so much. Regarding visual description, I am a white man, and not a millennial! I have gray hair, a gray beard, and tortoiseshell glasses. Thank you to the senior project advisor Rosemarie Garland-Thomson and to project codirector Joel Michael Reynolds, and thank you to you all for joining this sixth and final public conversation in our series. The purpose of this Hastings Center series is to broadcast and explore one fundamental theme: that people can flourish in all kinds of bodyminds. To "flourish" here means to exercise the capacities we have in pursuit of the purposes we find meaningful. We don't need different bodyminds to flourish. What we need is more supportive environments.

No one ever articulated our theme more powerfully than the late disability rights activist Adrienne Asch, who introduced the social model of disability to bioethics way back in the 1980s. Back in the 1990s, Adrienne and I led a project built around the bioethical dilemmas that arise when nondisabled people selectively abort fetuses based on disability status. Indeed, when Rosemarie, Joel, and I conceived of this in 2018, we felt that, to get at the project's fundamental theme, we would look at dilemmas that would resemble the ones that arose in the prenatal context. The original plan was for this final event in the series to return to the dilemmas that arise when people who are advocates both for reproductive choice and for disability justice contemplate using prenatal technologies. But over the course of the series, we felt ever less need to use a bioethical dilemma about a technology as an alibi for articulating our fundamental theme. We have become ever more eager to simply explore how disabled people can and do flourish within supportive environments.

In previous events, our speakers have reflected on their own ways of engaging in various activities that promote flourishing, including communicating, navigating, and enjoying. And today, instead of focusing on the prenatal dilemmas, we will focus on the activity or activities of family-making. This shift strikes me as important. There is a way in which using the prenatal testing dilemmas as the occasion for articulating our fundamental theme would place nondisabled people at the center of the conversation. It would have placed disabled people in the position of having to say things like, "You non-disabled people, in acting out of ignorance of what life without disability is like, are making an ethical mistake when you refuse to welcome babies with disabilities in your families."

Instead, today our event foregrounds the lived experience of disabled people and invites others to recognize its richness. We are saying, "Look here: this is a way in which disabled people are flourishing, making families, and expanding what it means to be in kinship with others."

We will hear three presentations today prepared by a total of six contributors. The creators of our first presentation, all of whom are professors of gender and women's studies, are Jina Kim, Jess Waggoner, and Sami Schalk. As many of you know, doulas support pregnant people as they bring babies into the world. Jina, Jess, and Sami will focus on what they call "queercrip doulaing," which refers to queer and transgender people with disabilities bringing young queer people into kinship with those people who share their identities.

The creators of our second presentation are Leah Smith and Joseph Stramondo. Joe is a professor of philosophy, and Leah is an activist. They will talk about what it is like to try to adopt children with disabilities like their own.

Mia Mingus will offer the third of our presentations. Mia is an educator and trainer for disability justice who will talk about the form of kinship that can grow around what she calls "access intimacy." Mia will speak about how having one's access needs recognized and recognizing the access needs of others can give rise to forms of kinship not dreamed of in the traditional model of the nuclear family.

Our aim today and throughout this series is to talk about disabled people flourishing. But this is not without its dangers. We might say about our conversation on family-making today something like what Julia Watts Belser said about the activity of enjoying. She said, "There are risks when we talk about joy, that we make joy a prescriptive, a requirement and a precondition for belonging." Julia continued, "There's a risk that the joy becomes another way of judging. If you are not happy, then you are doing it wrong." Plainly, today, that's the risk we intend to avoid. But it might be one that's of concern to people, and it is one that people are welcome to bring up in the audience discussion.

Jina Kim:

Hello everyone. Thank you all for coming. Our joint presentation is titled "Sustaining Queercrip Kinship in Pandemic Times." We will begin with a visual description of the presenters, and a content warning. This is Jina speaking. I am a Korean American woman, with glasses and frosted blonde tips. I'm wearing a Dalmatian sweater vest and a blue button-down shirt.

Jess Waggoner:

This is Jess Waggoner speaking. I am a white person with pink hair and pink lipstick, and I have a Dolly Parton pillow behind me and a Black Lives Matter sign. And my pronouns are they/them.

Sami Schalk:

Hi. I'm a fat Black woman with short curly hair, a teal dress with lace at the chest, and Lisa Frank glasses. And also there is a cat on my desk right now who might be in front of me during this talk.

Jina Kim:

Before we begin, we wanted to give content notifications for discussions of ableism and transphobia, and brief references to suicide. Please, do what you need to take care of yourself. Now, to begin, this is Jina reading.

In *Staying with the Trouble*, Donna Haraway urges readers to "make kin, not babies." Haraway's call reminds us of long-standing discussions in queer studies around family and affiliation beyond blood and biological relationships. But what does it mean for disabled people, in particular queer and trans disabled people, to make kin? And what does it mean to make kin when systems of heterosexism and white supremacy disrupt the life-sustaining ways we do create kin? And how can we love each other despite these systems that insist otherwise?

Finally, how do we forge these lines of intimacy during a pandemic, in which traditional ideas around family and household have fundamentally shaped discussions around public health and safety and collective responsibility? Driven by these questions, we want to share with you the ways we have learned to create and sustain kinship ties in and through practices grounded in disability and queer politics. For us, making queercrip kinship is not just about the "what" of it, but also about the "how"—that is, the practices we engage in in order to forge these ties. We define "queercrip kinship practices" as the things we do to create and sustain close relationships as queer and disabled people in ways that are akin to family-making, but that challenge traditional notions of what family is, means, or does. This is not a comprehensive overview: there are many, many ways to make queercrip kin, some of which disability scholars Alison Kafer and Shayda Kafai have described in their own writings on this topic.

For our presentation, we focus on the practice most relevant to us during the pandemic thus far, queercrip doulaing work.

We build on the work of disability justice activists Leah Lakshmi Piepzna-Samarasinha and Stacey Park Milbern, who coined the term "disability doulaing" to describe birthing and ushering people into a new disability identity. We issue a queercrip challenge to the concepts of family expansion, birth, and reproduction, especially within the context of a mass disabling event that might expand the ranks of those we consider queercrip kin.

We issue this challenge to address how the COVID-19 pandemic, and the suggested "best practices" for reducing viral transmission, have simultaneously reinforced and disrupted dominant understandings of family—that is, who "counts" as kin and the ways we connect with those who do count. In 2020, public health discourse framed friendship—and the practice of visiting friends or anyone outside of immediate family—as hazardous to collective safety, thereby elevating the isolated household as the pandemic gold standard.

As disabled queer people who live alone, rely on local community ties for survival, have robust chosen families, and maintain intentional distance from our families of origin, we felt particularly alienated by this set of recommendations that, to our minds, framed queer and nonfamilial ways of relating as potential threats of contagion. On the other hand, quarantine provided some relief to those of us looking to avoid our families of origin, especially during the holiday season, when feelings of obligation run high. All the while, we have drawn upon time-honored queer and crip strategies to maintain connection while living under systems of enforced isolation, which, we may add, queer and crip people have long endured. These strategies, such as long-distance and digital communication, helped us cultivate our chosen family networks at a time where touch and physical presence are not guaranteed.

Throughout our presentation, we draw on our personal experiences with queercrip doulaing with our "niblings." *Nibling* is an all-gender term we use to refer to the teens and children in our lives for whom we act as queer aunties, guncles (gay uncles), and fairy godparents. Some of our niblings have biological or legal connections to us and some do not, but they are all our niblings simply by existing in our lives and being in adult–child care relationships with us. Passing it on to Jess.

Jess Waggoner:

Thank you.
  Vignette one: Gay Bacon. E's message appears from the Discord server he created for us. "Gay bacon: voice chat, anyone?" A call across space and time for mundane virtual co-presence with queercrip results. At a time when sharing air has become an increasingly dangerous habit, these modes of connection are especially precious access technologies. We discuss the ways our particular disabilities gently shape or interfere with our desired gender presentations. Binders to flatten the chest that are accessible and low-pain can be out of reach for disabled trans people. Some masculine clothing, such as pants, is constricting and difficult to navigate with a disability. We elevate stretchy fabrics as a trans/crip revelation. I disclose that my desire to bind and wear more restrictive clothing has also helped me accept my disabled body as a trans body as is. We try on pronouns, discuss the possibility of keeping our names of origin, and generally exist in crip space, the familial neurodivergent rhythms of aimlessly hanging on video, the show and tell of objects in our space, sharing music and gushing over service dogs and ESAs (emotional support animals), between tough questions such as, "How do I really know I'm trans?"
  Under the mossy growth of pandemic temporalities, some young people have found the space to thrive. Others are isolated from their friends and queer kin, or trapped in unsupportive, oblivious,

or phobic family dynamics, dynamics which are indeed disabling. They witness the unfolding of harmful legislation targeting trans youth, and they question if they are indeed really trans. Some of them we have lost or are losing. This uptick in loss is linked to anti-trans legislation that invalidates trans youth, while the pandemic traps them in unsafe living situations. These bills send a message to trans youth that they should not exist, and impedes their access to life-saving care.

Vignette two: Cripping the Bisexual Chair Meme. As the pandemic reshapes many of our relationships with outdoor spaces, A, never an outdoor kid, will still design to sit outside in a camp chair and make absurdist queer art with me: *King of the Hill*'s Bobby Hill radiating rainbows, or propane tanks emblazoned against a queer flag. At eleven years old, A is a constant stream of self-educated, neurodivergent queer literacies, into which he weaves his love of '90s cartoons, despite the proliferation of current queer cartoons for young adults at his disposal. He prefers strange juxtapositions, queer takeovers, and reparative readings of media that are sometimes downright queer hostile.

As we listen to queer trans musician Cavetown gently destroy toxic masculinity—"Don't mess with me. I'm a big boy now and I'm very scary"—A is draping himself over the camp chair at the oddest angles, and I'm compelled to share with him the "bisexuals can't sit in chairs properly" meme. I joke to him that I am always already bi, because my pain levels make it so that I can never sit in a chair properly. Something clicks, and in communion with me, he is intentionally wrecking this chair with his contortions, reveling in the deep bi-ness of strange posture. This gentle playspace—instead of the blunt edge of asking, "What are you, how do you identify?"— this neuroqueer re-routing of gender, through revision, mystery, and absurdity, places us on a twisting path to the current moment, where he asks us to use a new name, and he/him pronouns, for the very first time. And now I am going to hand it off to Sami.

Sami Schalk:

This is Sami speaking.

Vignette three: Community Consultation. E has received a new disability diagnosis: hypermobility. The nurses at school send them home when his hip comes out of his socket, or call his brother to pop back in a shoulder. Wanting to help E with their practical access needs as well as this new disability identity, we connect him with a friend with a similar disability, a friend who is also trans, also queer. On a Saturday afternoon, we all hop on a Zoom call, E in their room with his mom who asks questions, takes notes. Our disabled, queer, trans friend works as an advocate and helps E and his mom prepare for an upcoming accommodation meeting with the school. But he also talks to E about mobility aids and the importance of being open to them, practicing with them, and learning which ones work best for one's body before there is a desperate need, an emergency. This queercrip doulaing conversation teaches about how to advocate for oneself, how to face internalized ableism and compulsory able-bodiedness, and shares the wisdom of the queercrip community. We all leave the conversation nourished, fortified by this connection, this process of bringing another person into the family. E begins to call the queer, trans, and disabled adults that we introduce him to his cousins, understanding these connections as forms of kinship long before we teach him the words we use to describe it. Welcome to the family, kiddo. We love you as you are. We welcome you as you are. There is a place for you here, with us.

The COVID-19 pandemic has taught us to move deeply with crip time, to revel in the joy of togetherness in whatever medium we find it, to deeply attune ourselves to one another's access vibrations, to remain open to our ever-shifting needs. Being a part of these conversations with our niblings has been healing for us. Every time, we think, What could we have done, who could we have been, if we had had a queer or disabled adult around to let us know we were perfect as we were, that we were going to be okay, someone who gave us words for our desires, for what was happening with our bodyminds? Loving our queer, trans, and disabled niblings is a way for us to love the young queer disabled people we were, who had to hide, who experienced so much shame and isolation, surrounded by biological family but completely without kin. Indeed, this process of queercrip doulaing is not a linear distribution of knowledge from elder queercrip to queercrip youth. Our niblings have shown us the power of vulnerability from queer, disabled adults. By allowing ourselves to be seen by them, and seeing them in turn, we have come to understand ourselves better.

Queercrip doulaing shows us that better queercrip worlds are possible. When people are connected to loving, safe community, including digital communities, where they can understand their identities, they don't have to experience the isolation, shame, stigma, or fear many of us have spent years undoing. We heal as we help, as we usher others into community, and into queercrip kinship. Thank you. I will hand it off to Leah and Joe.

Joseph Stramondo:

Hi, everyone. Thank you for that wonderful talk on queercrip kinship! That was so critical, important, and interesting. We will shift gears to talk about a more traditional view of family-making that nevertheless can be problematized and brought into conversation with some of these questions that were introduced in the first talk.

Leah Smith:

Let's do our descriptions first.

Joseph Stramondo:

Yes, before we get into the meat of our presentation, I will do an image description. I am a white man with dwarfism that has a dark beard and thinning dark hair. I am wearing round glasses and a white and blue checkered shirt buttoned up. We are sitting in a bedroom office.

Leah Smith:

I am Leah. I am sitting next to Joe. I have brown hair and glasses and a black top on. Behind us is a window and door.

Joseph Stramondo:

The name of our talk is called "Parenting While Disabled: From Eugenic Deficit to Disability Gain." The plan is to try to turn on its head the presumption that disability is a deficit or liability when being a parent.

I will start with some quick comments about the history of eugenics. We have the famous *Buck v. Bell* case, where Supreme Court Justice Oliver Wendell Holmes made his famous comment, "Three generations of idiots is enough." This case and others like it framed eugenics as relevant to the disability movement by focusing on this primary feature of historical eugenics: its emphasis on, "Who is fit to become a parent? Who is fit to raise children?"

Of course, eugenics isn't one thing. It's many things. But one of the prime pieces of eugenics was that it determined and tried to articulate what qualifies a person as a parent, and what qualities they should have if they are going to be good parents. It wasn't just about who was passing on what hereditary traits, but also the qualities of the parent. As you might know, the qualities of a good parent as articulated by the eugenics movement continue to the present day. They are still very common when thinking about what a good parent looks like or who a good parent is. We would like to suggest that some of these qualities can be traced back into the history of eugenics in the United States. In the eugenic view, good parents are, among other things, white, English-speaking, upper-middle class, heterosexual, and cisgender. They're people in traditional family roles. And of course, in this eugenic view, good parents are not disabled.

Leah Smith:

When we were creating the slide for this, I googled "good parent" to see what images showed up. The images I found all fit the description Joe just mentioned really well: white, upper-middle class, heterosexual and cisgender presenting, and nondisabled. They all uphold the idea of traditional family roles that can be traced back to the eugenics movement.

About a decade ago, *Rocking the Cradle*, which is a National Council on Disability report on disabled parents, came out. It revealed that there were a lot of common assumptions and biases against the ability of disabled parents. There was a disproportionately high rate of disabled people losing parental rights through the child welfare system. Of those, psychiatric disabilities were 70%–80% and intellectual disabilities were 40%–80%. Another finding was discrimination against disabled parents in custody or visitation disputes and also barriers for disabled parents to adopt children, domestically and internationally. Those barriers included violations of the ADA, discrimination by adoption agencies, and discrimination in international adoptions.

Joseph Stramondo:

There are additional ableist barriers that we thought worth mentioning. As we all know, access to healthcare generally is a real issue for many disabled people. They tend to be underemployed or unemployed. With the current situation in the United States especially, employment is tied to health insurance. There is a problem with reproductive healthcare and access for disabled people. Another barrier to parenthood is SSI (Supplemental Security Income) marriage penalties. This is where you lose benefits from the government if you get married. So, disability benefits can be put at risk by marriage. Certainly, marriage should not be a precondition to parenthood. But for many people, that is what they choose. We can see marriage penalties as a barrier to disabled people becoming parents.

Finally, there is the problem of inadequate access to technologies that assist people in being parents, such as cribs, strollers, and so forth. These are not usually made for disabled people and can be quite inaccessible. This is why, a lot of times, parents with disabilities need modified equipment that is often a rare find.

Leah Smith:

The image on the screen is a photo of, spoiler alert, our two kids. They are sitting inside of an accessible crib, which is a barn-door style crib that opens at the front so that we were able to reach them.

Joseph Stramondo:

It was difficult to come by. We were fortunate enough to be gifted it by another disabled parent from Minnesota. That's how difficult it is to get some of these technologies. It is not like you can pick them up at Target or have them gifted by your next-door neighbor.

I want to shift gears a little bit here and suggest that we ought not think about disability as a deficit or liability when it comes to parenting. To pick up on the theme of disability and the art of flourishing, let's talk about disability as a parenting gain. Here, we are using the term "disability gain." The term originates in the Deaf community, where it inverted the idea of hearing loss and instead talked about Deaf gain. "Deaf gain" was a term to refer to the value added to the world by Deaf culture and Deaf people. This term has been adopted more broadly beyond the Deaf community itself and is used by other disabled folk. Our claim is that the presumption that disability is a parenting deficit can also be inverted. We should think about the ways in which disability is actually a parenting gain.

Leah Smith:

First, let me tell you a little bit about our story. We met twelve years ago. We dated and were discussing our future, about family, and what we wanted that to look like. I fell in love with Joe because of his vision of family and how it matched mine. I didn't, and still don't, believe that disability is bad. I wanted to embrace that in our children as well. From the get-go, we had a strong desire to adopt a child with our same disabilities. We believe in the notion that disability is a gain in our parenting, and we felt we brought a different perspective to that than other parents. We went through the adoption process and went through two "failed" adoptions. In both cases, they were open adoptions. We built relationships with the moms especially before the adoption took place. The diagnosis for both children was dwarfism. In both cases, the mothers were confused by what that meant for them. It's safe to say there was a lot of fear. However, they went into the adoption process and got to know Joe and me.

Interestingly enough, as much as we wanted the adoptions to go through, in both situations we became so-called ambassadors of disability and what disability actually looks like. From two sets of biological parents that had never seen our kind of disability up close, they likely had lots of ableist ideas about what it would be like. After they got to know Joe and me, they both reversed their decisions. They decided that disability wasn't so bad after all. Of course, this wasn't fun for us. And it was a very expensive situation to go through in order to teach about disability parenting gain. What this really showed us was that we need better understandings of disability and parenting and what this looks like for people. It's not about who Joe and I are— it could have been anybody that could have taught them about life with dwarfism. It removed the fears and challenged the view of disability as a deficit and allowed them to imagine life with their child. It helped them see that what life would be like for their child couldn't be known from the diagnosis itself. It helped develop an understanding of disability as a neutral or even as a positive for them.

Joseph Stramondo:

We want to unpack this. The next step on our journey was the birth of our two bio kids. When we came up with the idea for this talk, we started kicking around ideas about what disability gain looked like as parents through our experience. Our experience is just a very narrow slice. I'm sure there are more examples of parenting disability gain. But we can give you a sense of what we have experienced here. There are, I think, two ways to think about parenting disability gain, or at least two sources of disability gain that we have experienced as parents. First, one can gain from disability as a social identity. In other words, we, as social persons who occupy a particular political position, offer our children a perspective they otherwise would not have. And, second, our bodies themselves offer to our children something they otherwise would not have.

But before we get to the embodiment piece, I want to say that sometimes I imagine what my life would be like had I been born average-sized and not acquired a spinal cord injury. When I think these thought experiments—and I'm a philosopher and we love our thought experiments—I think about how my perspective would have been so much more narrow, and . . . how, although I could have gotten to my current ideas about difference and inclusion, social justice, fairness, self-acceptance, interdependence, and so on and so forth, it would have been much harder without the lived experience of oppression. There's a stereotype or idea that disability is just there to teach nondisabled people a life lesson. That's something that disability activists often push back against, especially those looking at narratives in the media, saying, "We are not just here to teach lessons to nondisabled folks." I want to support that argument. However, there is a big exception to that rule. I think disability *should* exist to teach a moral lesson when you teach these lessons to your kids. Child-rearing is in fact a giant experiment in teaching moral lessons. So, if you could use disability as a resource—as Rosemarie Garland-Thomson might say—through parenting, it might open up the world to your children with respect to disability, inclusion, and difference. Hopefully, this will go beyond disability itself and apply to other marginalized identities and social justice in general. That would be a good thing, in my opinion.

Leah Smith:

The other parenting gain comes from disability as embodiment. We have seen this with our two kids. One, if you read any parenting article, the first thing they say is get at eye level with your kid in conflict or if you are framing a situation or redirecting. Something that's been positive for us, and a disability gain, is that we have been at eye level the whole time with our kids. I see a difference. I definitely see what a gain that has been for us. The other thing, as proponents for positive parenting, corporal punishment would not be an option for us ethically, even if we could do it physically. This presented a huge gain in helping us learn to use words only. There's no physical force. Our kids don't even know what that means. We also found that our kids have an understanding of bodily autonomy and consent more than some other children. In my case, most of my back is fused, and so I cannot wrestle. While wrestling is just the tip of it, they know they can't just jump on my back. They must be careful with me and always ask for consent with touch. Our youngest has often said, "Mommy is like a gentle flower." I love that in particular.

But it's an understanding that they must ask my consent with my body. I think that's important. And there's a greater sense of physical independence. When I got pregnant with our first and found out she would be average size, I was amazed by all the people that said, "How would you navigate that?! How will you teach her to ride a bike!? Or play on the playground?"

To be honest, we didn't know! We just knew we would figure it out! As the oldest, she has taught us so much, has navigated this on her own, and shown us what she can and will do without us prompting it. The bike riding is a good example. We waited for her to be ready to ride a bike without the training wheels. Last Christmas, we bought the bike, and we were like, "Okay, here goes!" Christmas morning, she got up, we went outside, she got on the bike, and just took off! That was the extent of us teaching her to ride without training wheels. The number of people that worried about this aspect of our parenting, but it was truly that simple. It was on her, and that's huge. We didn't push it. We waited for her. So, she really understands where her limits are and what her potential is.

Joseph Stramondo:

Expanding on the gains of parenting and embodiment itself, like I said in the beginning, all we have is our own experience to refer to here, but as I was coming up with this talk, another example occurred to me. There is a philosopher who teaches at Gallaudet University, Teresa Blankmeyer Burke—who gave one of the talks in the first event in this series—who reflected in another book chapter about how part of Deaf gain comes, not just from being part of Deaf culture, but from the particular form of embodiment that is deafness. An example of hers: when you are a parent and communicating with a child, as a Deaf parent, you must be very direct. You cannot communicate in a way that the child has divided attention. If you use lip reading or use ASL, or whatever the mode is that's specific to your family, you need to have all your focus on the child, and the child must have all their focus on you. It's not just an "uh-huh" from the kid as they play a video game. This is an example outside our own examples as Little People, but it's a disability gain focused on parenting that is worth noting.

And that's the extent of our talk! Oh yes, the image description.

Leah Smith:

Oh yes, the image description. Onscreen is an image of me and our youngest, sitting on my lap. We are wearing masks, but my lap is very full. Handing it off to Mia.

Mia Mingus:

Hi all. Thank you so much. I am going to talk about access intimacy. This talk is called "Building Our Own Belonging."

Disabled family-making can take many forms. It's not just the traditional nuclear parenting and child-raising—wait. Let me do a visual description. I'm a Korean American woman. I have a sleeveless black shirt on. My long hair is pulled back at the top only. I have large, white, shell-like . . . they look like moon earrings, on.

I'm sitting in a black office chair with a very, very boring white wall behind me, which I will paint at some point! It's just taking me a while. I have black glasses on too. Okay.

Disabled family-making takes many forms. It's not just the traditional nuclear parenting and child-raising. I want to talk about that more broadly, encompassing the many ways we are and become kin to each other as best friends, partners, comrades, or other loving relationships where we experience belonging, no matter how big or small. As a disabled queer adoptee of color, I understand family to be more expansive than we are taught. I have had my disability since I was an infant, my entire life. My physical disability has been visible and formal. I was marked as disabled by the medical industrial complex, which was an ever-present part of my childhood until I was eighteen. I understood myself to be disabled as far back as I can remember, and I was understood as disabled by everyone who met me. I was a disabled baby, child, and teenager, and these experiences profoundly and fundamentally shaped, and shape, how I understand disability.

In short, I haven't understood myself to be able-bodied or abled. I have only ever known a disabled life. This is a particular experience and life and culture that's distinct in the disability community. Disabled family-making has been one of the most powerful experiences of my life—"powerful" in its truest sense of a force that's able to cause effect. I say this because disabled family can be both world-altering, transformative, and transcendent, but also incredibly scarring and heartbreaking, and sometimes it can be both. I don't want to lose the harder parts of family-making when it doesn't work out or implodes or traumatizes.

Disabled people are so hungry for belonging and connection in a world that tells us we are wrong, undesirable, or a burden. These sentiments were internalized from a very young age. And for us all, no matter when we became disabled, these sentiments were widely understood and enforced. And of course, this is more compounded for those who are disabled with multiple oppressed identities.

Because of this hunger, we often rush forth with an intensity for connection. Many, myself included, are familiar with the crash-and-burn dynamics of these experiences. We so intensely yearn for relationships where we belong that when they fall apart, it can be nothing less than soul-crushing. Our longing for family is an ache. It's shaped by ableism and abled supremacy and isolation, loneliness, stigma, and inaccessibility. We live in a world that's not built for us. And the mere act of finding each other is hard, and learning how to move through the world together if our access needs conflict. We are sold family through a dominant culture that glorifies nuclear families and nuclear family-making. It says that family is the only place where belonging happens, even if that conflicts with our own experience in families without disabled children.

For most of us, our parents didn't know anything about disability outside of a medicalized understanding, or how to raise or support a disabled child. My family was not a place that could hold or cultivate disabled belonging. I share this because I don't want to romanticize disabled family-making. It can be magnificent, and it can also be painful. Some of my deepest heartbreak has come from family-making in disabled communities. The loss of disabled family has cut me to the bone. There are still wounds that throb when I think about them.

There is a deep contradiction that exists whenever we talk about disabled family-making, belonging, love, and community, because most disabled people do not have access to these communities. They do not have leaders with large, politicized communities. Or they have been ostracized from these communities, often pushed out by other disabled people. When we talk about disabled community, we must talk about envy and shame sometimes in these communities, even as it awakens longing, inspiration, and pride.

I think many of us have been on both sides of this. I want to acknowledge the quiet river of grief that moves through us in these conversations that is present alongside pride. Access intimacy has been a key part of a disabled need. Building a disabled family means to build an understanding of access intimacy and how it informs our lives, both in its presence and in its absence.

In my essay "Access Intimacy: The Missing Link," I describe access intimacy as the elusive, hard-to-describe feeling someone gets when someone understands your access needs. Sometimes it happens with complete strangers, disabled or not, or sometimes it is built over years. It can also be the way your body relaxes or opens up when someone understands your access needs. It doesn't require a political understanding of disability, ableism, or access. Some people have had no exposure or understanding to a political understanding of a disability. There are many ways ableism manifests in our lives.

Together, we share an experience with access intimacy that is ground-level. Instantly, we can hold the weight, emotions, isolation, fear, trauma, and anxiety of access. I don't have to justify and we are able to start from a place of steel vulnerability. It has taken the form of long talks into the night on a first meeting. Or the feeling of instant familiarity to be able to ask for support. It is an unspoken language between two people, like an entirely unique way of being able to communicate. Similar to meeting someone you just click with, access intimacy can take the form of an attraction, desire, or energy onto itself. There is no way to separate access from disability, no way to separate myself as a disabled person from my access needs. As I write, "In my life, access intimacy is something that has been hard won, organic, or at some times even felt magical. It has taken me by surprise, showing up with people that I never would have expected to have that kind of 'access connection' with. It has been exciting and relieving, like a long, slow exhale."

Access intimacy has felt like a kind of disabled belonging unto itself, a feeling of wholeness, as if I could take off my armor and be truly known. This is how family should feel. To be understood fully means that access intimacy is present. It is a familial experience, no matter the magnitude. Even in small moments it is impactful.

Once, I was traveling alone for work and getting off a plane with other disabled passengers while our mobility equipment was loaded onto a cart. I was the youngest person there. There was another woman who was ten years older than me, and three elders. We were to be whisked off to our respective gates. As we left the gate, a woman asked if she could use the bathroom. The driver flatly said, "No." She asked, "Please, sir," explaining how our flight was delayed and her connection was tight, so she would not be able to use the bathroom again until after her next flight, five hours later. Again, the man said, "No," this time a little more forcefully as the cart began to move. The woman was panicked when I spoke up and said, "She needs to use the bathroom. You have to let her." An elder waved his cane. I kept telling the driver to stop. The driver said, "Fine, I will let her, but I will not wait for her. It's her choice." The woman looked like she was going to cry, and the rest of us knew exactly how she felt. We stated that he should not drive away. We were yelling at him as gates flew by us and onlookers stared. Finally, spying the restroom, he pulled over and stopped. The woman got off the cart and thanked us through tears. Myself and one other elder stood with one leg on the cart and another off so that the driver could not move without hurting us. We waited there like that until she got back and we were all safely on board. We all talked and laughed. We were strangers when we got off that plane, but in that moment, we were family. We were a disabled family. We belonged with each other. We created belonging through shared access intimacy.

That experience stayed with me and opened up new space for possibilities. It was a small experience, but its roots ran deep. These moments leave me a little more whole, fortified, and nourished.

I had an experience with my current partner of eleven years. I experienced access intimacy when I met her. She had no previous experience with disability politics, but she supported me to write about it. She also became disabled in the last five years, and it has only enriched our shared intimacy as two disabled queer Koreans.

We have a relationship that is rooted in family and partnership. Access intimacy is both an integral part of building disabled family and a practice. Access intimacy is a recognition inside of me that is so deeply familiar. It is a part of me that has been lost and forgotten. It reminds me that there are other ways to exist beyond shame and fear. It reminds us of softness, care, and understanding. It is a generative force that embraces need. It creates new worlds and possibilities. Belonging can change us at a cellular level. There is no way to explain the alchemy of belonging and there is no formula to create it. For me, access intimacy has been a building block of disabled belonging, and a path to family. I only wish that I had been able to experience access intimacy as a disabled child as the ableist world swirled around me. I dream that future generations of disabled children will be able to experience belonging born out of chosen family and forged out of access intimacy. Thank you. I will turn it back to you all.

Rosemarie Garland-Thomson:

Thank you very much for those wonderful presentations. I am Rosemarie Garland-Thomson. I am a pale-skinned, senior-ish woman with red glasses. I am joining you today from my home office in San Francisco. I want to offer one question about relatedness and resemblance. We have all noted, after the last number of years, that calls for inclusion invoke an idea that people want to have more "people who look like me" in their lives. I thought about how that might work with disability kinship in terms of resemblances and relatedness. I want us to talk to each other about the relationship between kinship circles and relatedness and resemblance. For the people who identify as disabled and who are identified as disabled, how we might resemble each other or look like each other, how we might be biologically similar, whether it's through genetic, morphological, and biological relatedness, or through relatedness that has to do with our minds as well as our bodies. How do the distinctive resemblances and likenesses help us forge more meaningful kinship networks? I hope we can talk about likeness, resemblance, and how it operates specifically in disability kinship circles. Joe and Leah, do you want to talk, since you talked about the contrast between resemblance and looking like your children, and maybe even looking like and not like one another? And maybe the rest of us can follow in.

Joseph Stramondo:

Wow, okay. I have been thinking about this question. I think it is a really interesting and risky question to ask. I think there is something there. There is something about disability embodiment that creates a tendency toward access intimacy, as Mia was talking about. I do think that experiencing disability, for me, makes me more likely perhaps to put into the foreground access intimacy with others. I am thinking about a set of experiences I had with our mutual friend, the late Stacey Park Milbern. One time, when we were meeting up in Washington, DC, we were going to get on the metro together, two power chair users. I dropped my metro card on the ground. Of course, she couldn't help me pick it up. While I was climbing out of my chair, she immediately parked her chair in front of me so people could not see me climb out of my chair. She intuitively knew that being out of my chair, I was vulnerable. Being in my chair was a source of independence and power. Being out of my chair would be too much intimacy for the people around me who were not Stacey.

I think about how the space of access intimacy is created with the intuitive understanding of our commonality and experiences. But—and here is a big "but"—I don't want to oversell that. There is a lot of hierarchy in the disability community. Especially as a cis-het, white, upper-middle-class man, I have to be attuned toward that hierarchy. And that's another lesson that Stacey Park Milbern taught me: disability is not a unified monolith. There is difference within difference, and I have to recognize my own privilege and power in my body. I must not flatten the experience of disability to a fairytale commonality that does not exist. So that's my answer.

Leah Smith:

I had a conversation with my five-year-old the other day. Out of the clear blue she said, "Do you know the ways that we are the same and different?" and I said, "What's that?" I obviously can think of quite a few ways that we're different and ways that we're the same. And she said, "We are the same because we have the same eyes, we are both kind, and we both like to put outfits together." I said, "Yes—that is true." Then she said, "Do you know how we are different?" And she said, "You have purple nail polish on. I don't." I thought, wow, of all the things she could have said in that moment, she thought of purple nail polish. But on a deeper level, Joe and I deal with this a lot when we are out. We are both Little People, but we are different types of Little People. We often laugh about how people interact with us and how different people are with us. His wheelchair is the first thing people see. They don't actually pay attention to anything else. My body is the first thing that they notice with me. Some of it is sexism, some of it is gender. There are a lot of things at play. Those are the two thoughts that came to my mind when you asked that.

Sami Schalk:

I have a nonapparent disability. For me, recognizing kin is not through the body at all. Sometimes it is about the things people are doing, not just the bodies themselves. I am thinking about that.

I am a mixed-raced person who was raised by white people, and so, for me, kinship has never been about seeing people who look like me, because I was not raised by people who look like me and I was often assumed not to be part of the family. I would watch little cousins and people would think I was a hired babysitter. For me, kinship is about the shared connection and experiences that we have. It is important in disability and crip kinship because what we share is often about how the world treats us regardless of the ways our bodies appear.

Jess Waggoner:

Jess speaking. I wanted to reflect on what was just said, and the experience of trans disabled people. We have to leverage pathology or diagnosis to strategically access gender-affirming care, but sometimes we don't have access to diagnosis or services in the first place. I understand all these identities overlapping because of the disabling conditions that trans people face every day. For many reasons, disabled trans people don't visually recognize one another. And that can be because of safety and how we can't present in the ways we want to, or because of preexisting disabilities or medical trauma that shapes the forms of care we can access or want to access, or a place where we don't want to change our presentation at all! So we have to generate different ways to find each other. Like virtual spaces or a glance, or a shift in tone. But that's one potential trans or crip ethic: to not just use the visual to find each other.

Mia Mingus:

Mia speaking. I wanted to add, so many things that others said were things that came up for me. One more piece. I think for me, even if I do recognize someone as being disabled or a fellow crip or fellow gimp, that's one piece of it. I think language plays a big part in recognizing, especially if their disability is not visible or obvious. But there's also this piece where that is just descriptively recognizing somebody. But that doesn't necessarily mean that they have a disabled identity, politicized or not—that they understand themselves as disabled. I have met so many, in particular, women of color who are visibly disabled—whom anybody would recognize as disabled according to the tiny, narrow, terrible understanding of disability that exists in the predominant paradigms. But so many of those folks didn't identify as disabled, even if they were using a power chair, for example. It connects to stigma as well as having multiple oppressed identities. And if you are oppressed by gender or race, identifying as disabled can threaten your survival. And this relates to how we find each other. I have conversations with these folks, and they know what it means to live a disabled life, but they don't identify as such.

Sami Schalk:

Mia, what you said reminds me of something attributed to Zora Neale Hurston, but it's a community Black saying: "Not all skin folk are kin folk." Not everyone that looks like me is kin. I have met queer folk and I'm like, "Oh, we are not in community! We are in very different places in terms of our understandings of our queerness." That is clear to me with disability, too. Other people in the queer community or the disabled community can break our hearts.

Mia Mingus:

I want to respond to your second question, Rosemarie. Yes, there is the kind of new-world-making or meaningful connections within subcultures under the large umbrella of *the* disabled community. But also, when you find people where your access needs are different, but they really complement each other, that can be also world- and life-altering. I can't walk long distances, but folks in power chairs can just zip down to the corner and get something for us that we need and come right back. That is its own special kind of other-world-making in disability community.

Rosemarie Garland-Thomson:

I have an ongoing project with two of our colleagues in the disability community, one of whom is blind, and the other of whom is Deaf. I have crippled, mobility impairment, however you want to talk about it—and the interdependence of working on things together or traveling together is really very moving. The way that we have developed expertises in using the world, and the way we work with one another to be a unit, a trio, a triangle of weird women or witches—as you have all suggested, in our chosen communities, it's very moving and surprisingly effective to the rest of the world.

Joel Michael Reynolds:

I'm a white person wearing glasses and a burgundy shirt that matches my nails. I made sure I was matching. I have tattoos, and I'm sitting in a chair in my apartment that's blurred a bit, but not enough! We have fantastic questions from the audience: "What can you do if parent groups take over your local disability community and advance proposals that contradict what actual disabled people want, for example, promoting a disability registry with local police instead of alternative crisis responses?" Would anyone like to respond to that question?

Sami Schalk:

This is Sami. I don't have this experience. But in thinking about other organizing communities that I belong to, there's not just one community. We say "disability community" or "queer community." But that's not only the case. So it's okay to say, "You know what, you do that, and we will do this thing over here!" Allow people to come in and be a part of it. I would challenge the idea of taking over. Just say you will go do something different. I understand that's hard when the thing they are advocating for is harmful. And it's okay to be clear about that and that you believe that. But in a singular local community, it's okay to take different directions of what people want to do, or to take on different organizing work. Or educating people. But it's not your job to educate everyone.

Leah Smith:

It should be noted that there's often a tension between parents without disabilities and adults with disabilities. So, as a disabled person, I feel I'm right! But I'm also a parent. So, I understand the need to protect your child. But to push the narrative of our firsthand experience and of our understanding being the only legitimate way of approaching an issue can be harmful. I hope we wouldn't do this in other marginalized communities that we are at the edges of and that our children may belong to. I know that's oversimplified. But I want to acknowledge that tension that happens in these groups.

Joseph Stramondo:

To speak to Sami's point, that's a powerful and good point in so far as just not getting too worked up about it. Instead, just doing your own work, and going and doing your own thing, I think that's a really effective strategy. I have seen that happen in various disability communities across the country. Folks were doing something problematic, and instead of confronting or fighting them, you organize in your own way with your own goals. But the limit to that is when the struggle exists in a single institution. I have experienced this, where there might be an advocacy organization with these tensions present. So, there is a kind of institutional struggle for the soul of the organization, so to speak. You have groups pitted against each other in a single structure. You would then lose something to leave and start your own thing. I think you need to be careful with thinking to yourself, "Is it worth it?" Is it worth it to have this fight in this particular structure for its mission? Or should I set out and do my own thing, and not spend this energy on this particular fight?

Joel Michael Reynolds:

Thank you so much for all those responses. Another question from the audience: "I would love to hear your thoughts on how we can make queercrip space for those with intellectual and developmental disabilities. I don't see crossover in our community to make our movement accessible for those with different levels of cognitive ability or communicative skill."

Jess Waggoner:

Jess speaking. I can offer what I have done, but I'm excited to hear what others have to say. With community work, I think we can start with urging queer and trans community centers and groups and social services and events to center accessibility for all disabled people. The way to do this on the macro is to offer to attend or generate listening sessions for the boards of these community centers. They often think about elder care in terms of disability access, but not cross-generationally or across disabilities. Or offer workshops on intersectionality for these boards and on queerness and other identities. And that access will draw in more people and allow us to recognize that so many queer and trans people are already disabled.

Rosemarie Garland-Thomson:

In response to the question about creating accessible community for people with cognitive and neurodiversity, I am working on projects that hope to translate some of the work on disability studies into plain language. We are working with a bunch of people to translate the *New York Times* articles on disability from *New York Times* language into plain language. So that's one important piece of work in terms of disability access, in terms of language.

Mia Mingus:

I want to add to this. This is Mia, and I don't know where this lives. I also think that really having queer and trans spaces confront these politics is key for making these spaces more accessible. I think it is good to confront the need to be desirable. A lot of those spaces function as spaces to cruise, find dates, get laid, or find hookups. I don't know the language kids are using today, so I am dating myself. But I think that that's a huge part of the stigma and the accessibility around folks who have different kinds of communication skills, whatever their abilities may be, or however that may manifest. I know that is a very hard thing to do. I think a lot of queer and trans culture is built around being desirable, so it might also mean that we think about what it means to be queer and trans and how we can do that in a nonableist way.

Joel Michael Reynolds:

We have way more questions than we can possibly answer. We encourage you to reach out to our speakers, reach out to us in social media or whatnot. We always save the questions in the chat and send them to our speakers. By no means do we want this conversation to end. This is just an opening. We have time for at least one or two more questions: "This has been an incredible event. Do you have experience with prenatal testing and how it impacts disability justice? Given how routinely testing is being implemented, sometimes without a pregnant person's knowledge, how can we incorporate disability and reproductive justice in a wider set of practices? Is it even compatible with such equity and inclusion principles?"

Joseph Stramondo:

I will do my best. I think that this is the tension Erik mentioned in the beginning, the motivation behind this discussion. I think it is relevant to what we spoke of today. I am going to try to address this in the spirit of today's event and the spirit of this whole series and say, that, well, the problem is more fundamental than the technology itself. The technology is, yes, problematic, but it is something that has been created by a deeply ableist culture. Recognizing the technology and doing some kind of public education campaign focusing on the technology itself is not going to do the work. The problem is, ableism existed earlier in human history than the discovery of the genome. An approach is to, yes, write and think about biotechnology, but we have to do this with the understanding that we are embedded in a deeply ableist culture. It is within the intersection of racism, sexism, et cetera. These drive these technologies in the first place. I know this is a nonanswer, but it might be the best that I can do.

Jina Kim:

I wanted to add that I think this would also be a great place to consider how reproductive justice has deeply thrown into question the framework of choice that often has driven the reproductive freedom conversation. I think Joe explains beautifully how choice is not in a vacuum. It is shaped by broader systems of ableism. It makes it unthinkable for parents to believe they could raise a child with a disability. I think the critique of the choice framework is applicable here as well.

Sami Schalk:

This is Sami. Some of my work is on speculative fiction. When I speak of this, I talk about how technology is a tool which is not inherently good or bad. I can imagine a world where genetic testing is used so that parents know about their forthcoming child's disability. They are connected to their community and are prepared to raise these children. All of these other things around the technology, and not just the tool itself, matters. This is a way and hope that technology could be included in a just world. It could, but all these other things would have to change.

Mia Mingus:

I think this is a both/and. I don't think there are any easy answers. I think when we get into the topic of reproductive genetic technologies and that world, we have to remember we exist in a world with binaries. There are more complexities. I don't think there is something wrong with prenatal testing, but because of the entire world of reproductive technologies, that world is moving faster than the laws can catch up with. Who cares about laws, I know, but that's all we have to help to monitor it. I think it's a slippery slope and there are no easy answers. As a disabled person who worked in the reproductive justice movement, I think we live both and/or lives. We can understand these things in positive ways. I want us to also understand all the nuance.

Joel Michael Reynolds:

I want to highlight a book edited by Erik Parens and Josephine Johnston entitled *Human Flourishing in the Age of Gene Editing*, which has some fantastic resources that address this directly, including by our own Rosemarie Garland-Thomson. I also want to highlight an essay that I love by Joseph Stramondo: "Disability and the Damaging Master Narrative of an Open Future." Before we run out of time, I want to ask a final question. This question comes from our own Liz Bowen. Liz asks, "Mia's reflection on the quiet river of grief really resonated with me. There is a tragedy that these relationships, which are crucial to survival in the face of ableism, can also buckle under the weight of the same failures of social and material support. What do you think will need to most change structurally to lessen us crashing and burning, as Mia puts this?"

Mia Mingus:

I can start. You know, it is funny, because I don't often think about structural things when I am thinking about the formations that happen around belonging and disabled family-making, because they oftentimes happen outside of those structures. I think that community infrastructure could really help, that's less formal. One where we can actually have communities, where we don't just talk about that. I don't want it to be only the few popular folks who have access to community. It should not be homogeneous either. I think, right now, there is a push for de-institutionalization. We want to get disabled folks out of the institutions. I know we can't guarantee people that there won't be harm or violence if we take them out of institutions. Our communities are so messed up as well. I think that having broader communities, like queer and trans people of color communities, for example, can contend with ableism. It can build cross-disability relationships but also relationships that are not only in disability community. I think about how disabled people can have access to mental health, to heal trauma. There are so many pieces. Our trauma as disabled people is one of the biggest causes of the crash-and-burn dynamics, as well as those larger structures. They're interdependent and connected.

Erik Parens:

On behalf of my collaborators Liz Bowen, Rosemarie Garland-Thomson, and Joel Michael Reynolds, I want to thank today's speakers for sharing their generous, incisive, and generative thoughts. And once again, thanks to our program officer at the National Endowment for the Humanities, Patricia Brooks, without whose support this series would not have happened.

Notes

Introduction

1. See Erik Parens and Adrienne Asch, eds., *Prenatal Testing and Disability Rights* (Georgetown University Press, 2000); Joel Michael Reynolds and Christine Wieseler, eds., *The Disability Bioethics Reader* (Routledge, 2022), Adrienne Asch, "Disability, Bioethics, and Human Rights," in *Handbook of Disability Studies*, eds. Gary L. Albrecht, Katherine D. Seelman, and Michael Bury (SAGE Publications, 2001); Rosemarie Garland-Thomson, "The Case for Conserving Disability," *Journal of Bioethical Inquiry* 9 (2012): 339–355; Jackie Leach Scully, *Disability Bioethics: Moral Bodies, Moral Difference* (Rowman & Littlefield Publishers, 2008); Anita Silvers, David T. Wasserman, and Mary Briody Mahowald, *Disability, Difference, Discrimination: Perspectives on Justice in Bioethics and Public Policy* (Rowman & Littlefield Publishers, 1998); Joseph Stramondo, "How Disability Activism Advances Disability Bioethics," *Ethical Theory and Moral Practice* 25 (2022): 335–349.
2. Hannah E. Davis, Lisa McCorkell, Julia Moore Vogel, and Eric J. Topol, "Long COVID: Major Findings, Mechanisms and Recommendations," *Nature Reviews Microbiology* 21, no. 3 (March 2023): 133–146, https://doi.org/10.1038/s41579-022-00846-2.

Chapter 1

1. Erik Parens, *Shaping Our Selves: On Technology, Flourishing, and a Habit of Thinking* (Oxford University Press, 2015).
2. Teresa identifies herself so that blind participants/audience members will know who is speaking.

Chapter 2

1. Nancy Mairs, "On Being a Cripple," in *Plaintext* (University of Arizona Press, 1986).
2. Andrew Harnish, "Ableism and the Trump Phenomenon," *Disability and Society* 32, no. 3 (2017): 423–428, https://doi.org/10.1080/09687599.2017.1288684.
3. Rosemarie Garland-Thomson, *Extraordinary Bodies: Figuring Physical Disability in American Culture and Literature* (Columbia University Press, 1996).
4. Sins Invalid, "10 Principles of Disability Justice," https://www.sinsinvalid.org/blog/10-principles-of-disability-justice.
5. Talila Lewis, "Ableism," https://www.talilalewis.com/blog/working-definition-of-ableism-january-2022-update.

Chapter 3

1. Margaret Price, "The Bodymind Problem and the Possibilities of Pain," *Hypatia* 30, no. 1 (2014): 268–284.
2. Susan Schweik, *The Ugly Laws: Disability in Public* (New York University, 2009).
3. Bureau of Labor Statistics, US Department of Labor, *Persons with a Disability: Labor Force Characteristics—2019* (2020).
4. Jill Magi, "Ecopoetics and the Adversarial Consciousness." *The Eco-language Reader* (Portable Press/Nightboat Books, 2011).

Chapter 4

1. Cathy A. Malchiodi, *Trauma and Expressive Arts Therapy: Brain, Body, and Imagination in the Healing Process* (The Guilford Press, 2020); Cathy A. Malchiodi, *Art Therapy Sourcebook* (McGraw-Hill, 2006).
2. Ann Millett-Gallant, *Re-Membering: Putting Mind and Body Back Together Following Traumatic Brain Injury* (Wisdom House Books, 2017).
3. Rudi Coetzer, *Anxiety and Mood Disorders Following Traumatic Brain Injury: Clinical Assessment and Psychotherapy* (Karnac Books, 2010).
4. *My Beautiful Broken Brain*, directed by Sophie Robinson and Lotje Sodderland (Netflix, 2014).

Chapter 5

1. For more information about *We Run Like Rivers*, see https://www.clairecunningham.co.uk/event/we-run-like-rivers/.